14 Pi Ra

Young People's Science Encyclopedia

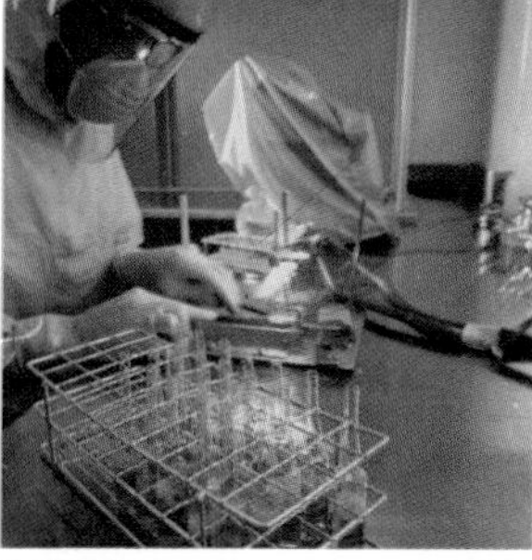

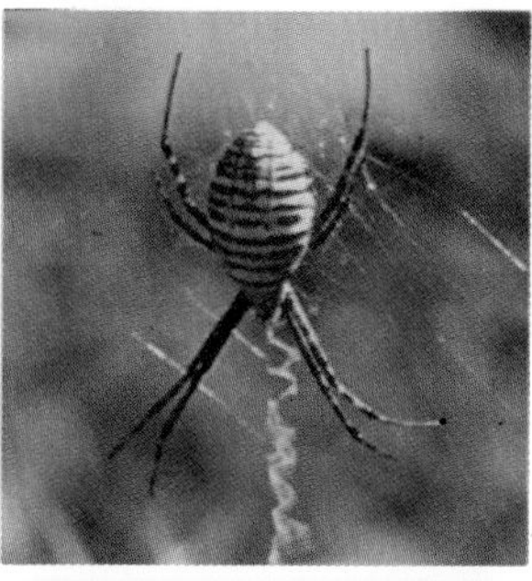

YOUNG PEOPLE'S SCIENCE ENCYCLOPEDIA

Edited by the Staff of
NATIONAL COLLEGE OF EDUCATION, Evanston, Illinois

Young People's SCIENCE Encyclopedia

Edited by the Staff of

NATIONAL COLLEGE OF EDUCATION

Evanston, Illinois

Volume 14/Pi-Ra

CHICAGO

Photographs

Page 2: Skylab space station (NASA)

Page 3: *Top to Bottom:*
Wheatfield (U.S.D.A. Photo)
Technician capping Abbokinase (Abbott Laboratories)
Spider (Macmillan Science Company)
View of Earth (NASA)
Space Shuttle (NASA)
Bahama coral reef (Macmillan Science Company)

Cover: Design by Sandra Gelak
Close-up of the Moon (NASA)
Goose Lake Prairie State Park (James P. Rowan)
Porpoise Show: Brookfield Zoo (James P. Rowan)

Library of Congress Catalog Card Number: 67-17925

Published simultaneously in Canada.

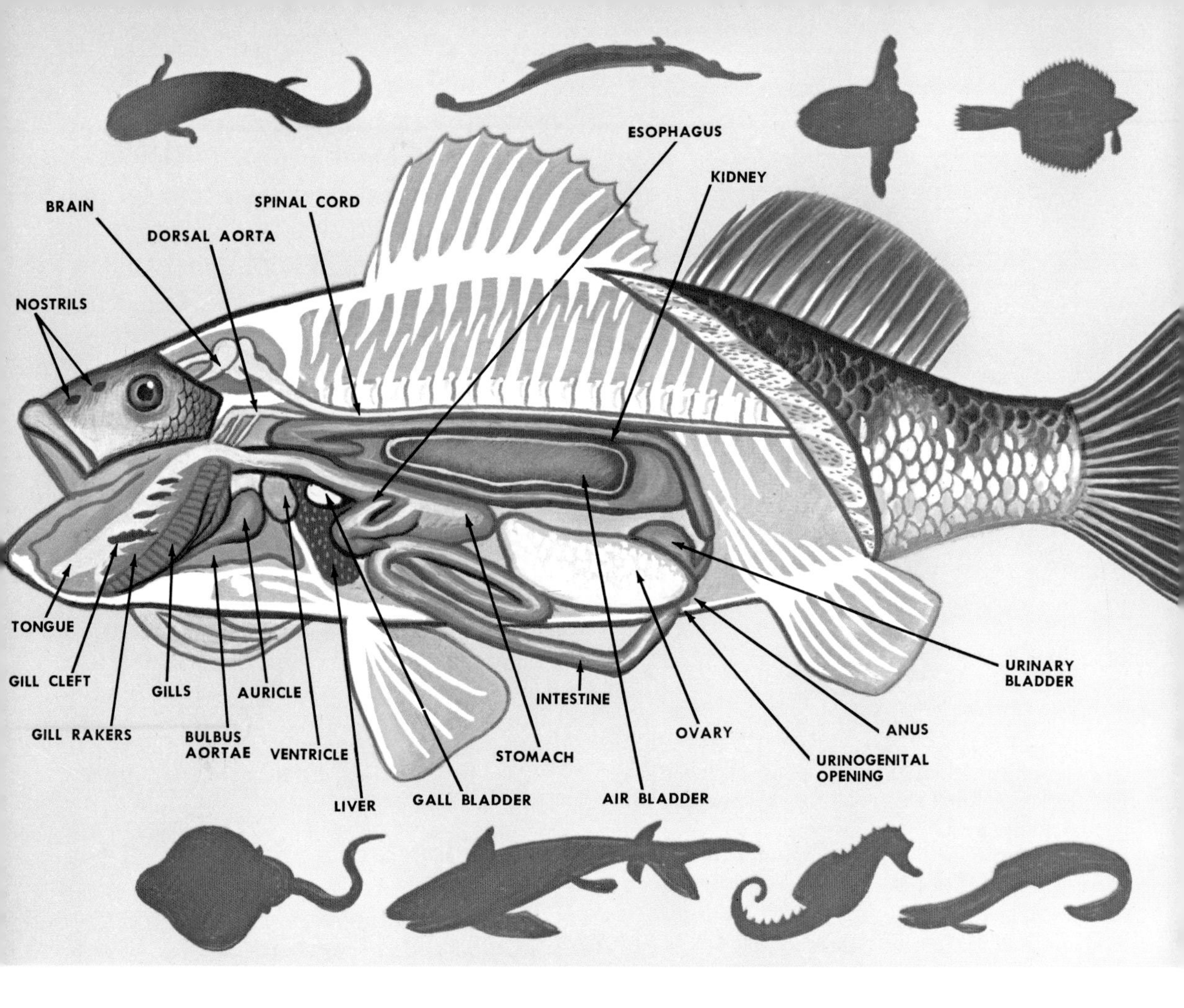

Pisces (animal) (PIH-ceez) Pisces means fish. The class of VERTEBRATES that included all of the fish was formerly called Pisces. Pisces is often dropped as a scientific name. All fish live in water. They are an old group. Fish first appeared in the *Silurian* period, over four hundred million years ago, and became so plentiful that the next period, the *Devonian,* is called the Age of Fishes.

Besides the many types of fish that have become extinct, there are about 13,000 living species. Among the vertebrates there are three classes of fish. One class includes jawless fish like LAMPREY EELS and hagfish. The other two classes are made up of jawed fish. SHARKS, SKATES, BASS, and PERCH are examples of fish in this group.

All fishlike creatures are not fish. SEALS, DOLPHINS, PORPOISES, and WHALES are fishlike in form, but they are MAMMALS. They breathe with LUNGS and nurse their young with milk glands. Flippers are used for swimming instead of fins.

Jawless fish are placed in the class Agnatha which includes the lamprey eels and hagfish. These primitive fish have unpaired fins, no scales, and round, sucker-like mouths that are equipped with horny ridges for tearing flesh.

Jawed fish with skeletons made of CARTILAGE and paired fins are in the class Chondrichthyes. Sharks and RAYS belong in this class. The members of the second class of jawed fish have bone skeletons and paired fins. They are called Osteichthyes. PIKE, perch, TROUT, bass, *tuna,* and many others are bony fish. These fish have swim bladders and gill coverings called *opercula.*

Both bony and cartilaginous fish are scaled. The scales of the shark group are embedded in the skin and are called *placoid scales.* They are replaceable and thought to be evolutionary forerunners of mammalian teeth. The scales of bony fish, called *ganoid scales,* are on the surface of the skin and overlap like roof shingles. When they are lost, they do not grow again. The structure of ganoid scales is

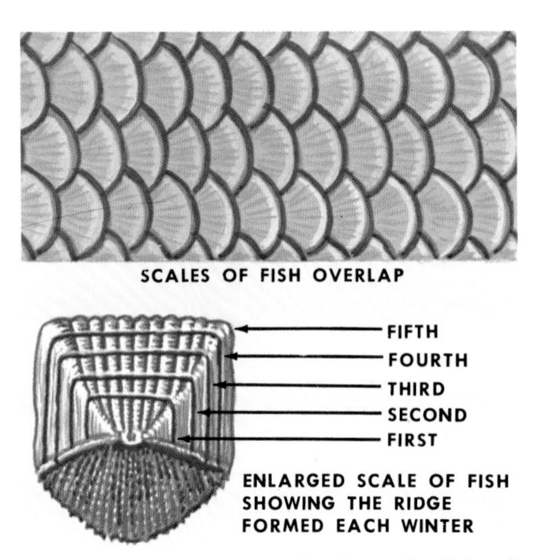

The age of scaly fish can be determined by the ridges on the scales

like that of placoid scales, but ganoid scales appear on the skin surface in diagonal rows of platelike armor.

The fins in the cartilaginous fish are covered with skin and are supported by rays of cartilage Pectoral and pelvic (ventral) fins are paired. Tail, dorsal, and anal fins are not paired. The anal fin, near the opening of the digestive tract, is either lacking or modified to transfer sperm. Bony fish have fins similar to those of cartilaginous fish, but they are transparent and supported by bony rays that may be soft or stiff and spiny. Many species in this class have fins that have been modified in shape and position.

In both classes of jawed fish, forward speed is controlled by the tail. The pectoral fins usually control direction of movement while dorsal and anal fins stabilize movement.

DIGESTIVE SYSTEMS of fish are complete. Esophagi are short and stomachs usually J-shaped. *Circulation* is accomplished by a two-chambered heart through which the blood flows only once per circuit. *Respiration* is by gills. Slits in the pharynx bear thin vascular filaments or gills. Most ENDOCRINE GLANDS are present; however, in lampreys the PANCREAS is missing. The PARATHYROID is lacking in all fish. Most fish have frog-type KIDNEYS, although in lampreys the kidneys are more primitive. Sexes are usually separate. Fish can be OVIPAROUS or sometimes OVOVIVIPAROUS. J. C. K.

SEE ALSO: ANIMALS, CLASSIFICATION OF; FISH; LAMPREY EEL; SHARK

Pisces (constellation) (PIH-ceez) Pisces is a group of stars that form a pattern or picture in the sky called a CONSTELLATION. Pisces, one of many constellations, is an autumn constellation; it can best be seen on a clear, moonless night during that season in the Northern Hemisphere. Its stars are faint compared to the stars that form some of the other constellations.

People of ancient civilizations imagined that the stars of Pisces formed a pattern that resembled two fish. The two fish are far apart, and each is made up of a group of faint stars roughly in the shape of a diamond. It can be imagined that the two fish are joined together by their tails by long ribbons outlined by stars. At the end the ribbons form a knot shown by a comparatively bright star. The whole constellation takes the form of an extended and straggling V.

Pisces is one of the twelve signs in the *zodiac*. It is in the last or twelfth position. This is the time of the vernal equinox, or the first day of spring when the sun appears to cross the celestial equator. H. S. G.

SEE ALSO: CONSTELLATION, ZODIAC

Pisces, the Fishes

Pistachio see Nuts

Pistil (PISS-till) The pistil is the center part of a female FLOWER. A pistil is made of three parts: a base or *ovary*, a tube or *style*, and a sticky end or *stigma*. A pistil may be single or compound. It is frequently attached to the upper end of the flower stalk or receptacle.

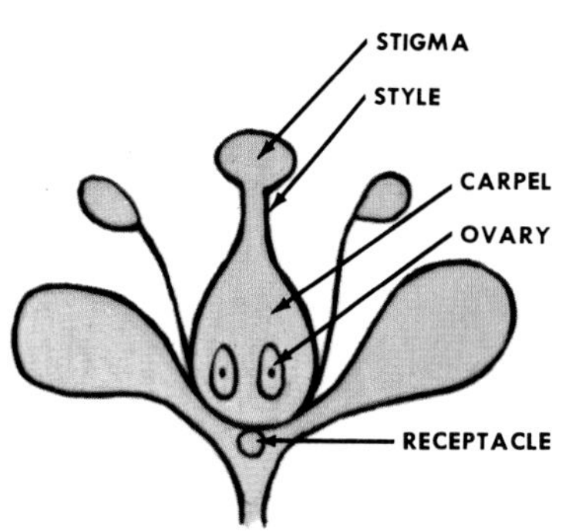

The pistil (female part) of a flower

POLLINATION and FERTILIZATION occur on and in the pistil. Following these processes, the ovary may mature into a FRUIT with seeds. Compound pistils have more than one chamber or carpel.

Imperfect flowers (flowers that do not have both male and female parts in a single flower) are either pistillate or staminate. Immature ears of corn are pistillate flowers. Each flower on the willow catkin is nothing more than a pistil. H. J. C.

Piston see Automobile, Engine

Pitch see Resonance, Sound

Pitchblende Pitchblende is the mineral which is the chief commercial source of URANIUM and RADIUM. It is brown or black, streaked with green, and dull in appearance except for freshly broken surfaces which have a faint luster and a greasy look.

In its pure form pitchblende is an oxide of uranium, formula UO_2; but it usually contains lead and small amounts of other elements, including radium. There are many varieties of pitchblende, each made up of a different combination of ELEMENTS.

Pitchblende is found in Czechoslovakia, England, Norway, and many other European countries and in several parts of the United States. It is nonmagnetic, brittle, and has a specific gravity varying from 6.4 to 10.6. E. R. B.

SEE ALSO: CURIE, MARIE AND PIERRE; RADIOACTIVE ELEMENTS

Pitchblende

Courtesy Society For Visual Education, Inc.

Insects fall down the tubes of pitcher plants and cannot escape

Pitcher plant The pitcher plant is an *insectivorous* flowering plant. This means that it is an insect-eating plant. There is a family of pitcher plants which are large and showy and grow in most marshy parts of the United States and Canada.

The pitcher plant has tubular, yellow-green leaves, brightly marked with deep red and purple veins which attract the insects. Fine hairs pointing downward grow at the mouth of the pitcher. The sweet smell of nectar at the rim of the leaf lures the insects into the leaves; then the hairs help to prevent the insect from crawling out where the walls are smooth and slippery. The insects fall to the bottom where there is water, and there they are trapped and digested by the plant. However, this plant still receives most of its food supply by PHOTOSYNTHESIS.

A single purplish flower grows at the end of a tall stem. While pitcher plants belong to several genera of two different families, those in genus *Sarracenia* are most widely distributed. The common name of the pitcher plant varies locally. J. K. K.

SEE ALSO: PLANTS, INSECTIVOROUS

Pith Pith is the tissue found in the center of young stems. The cell's walls are thin. Pith functions primarily as a food storage tissue.

Certain plants have pith strong enough to put to a special use. The pith of rushes, for example, was used for wicks in candles and lamps. M. R. L.

SEE ALSO: PLANT TISSUES

Pitot tube see Altimeter

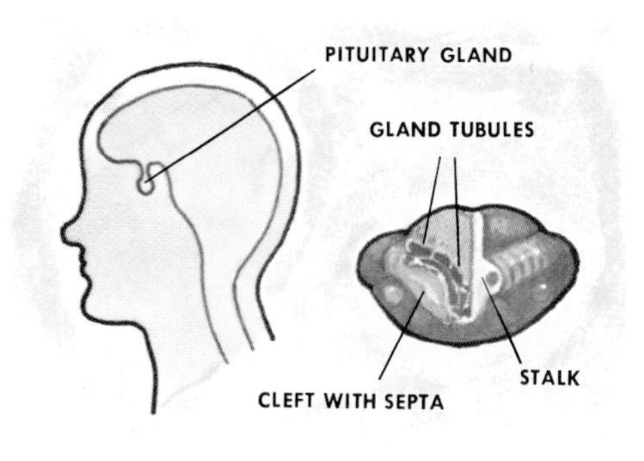

Pituitary gland (pih-TOO-ih-tairy) The pituitary is a small gland on the undersurface of the BRAIN. In spite of its size, it is sometimes called the "master gland." It has an influence on almost every part of the body. It is controlled by the NERVOUS SYSTEM and controls other glands, including the sex glands (GONADS).

The pituitary gland has three main parts. The front part is called the *anterior lobe* or *adenohypothysis*. The rear portion is called the *posterior lobe* or *neurohypothysis*. A narrow middle area where the two parts meet and fuse is called the *intermediate lobe*. The gland is attached to the brain by a stalk known as the *infundibulum*.

The posterior lobe secretes *neurohormones*. These are proteins that seem to have five functions. They contract the muscles in the milk glands, causing milk ejection; they contract the SMOOTH MUSCLES of the *uterus;* they act on the kidney to prevent excess loss of water; they contract smooth muscles in the walls of blood vessels, causing a rise in blood pressure; and they regulate the release of anterior lobe HORMONES.

The intermediate lobe is prominent in infants and present in all VERTEBRATES except the WHALE, ARMADILLO, and Indian ELEPHANT. In some vertebrates, pigment cells are controlled by hormones produced in the intermediate lobe. Among fish and reptiles, pigment dispersion or concentration in the branched pigment cells (*chromatophores*) is regulated by the nervous system or by the nervous system and hormones. AMPHIBIAN chromatophores are controlled by hormones, but the secretion of the hormones is under nervous control. In BIRDS and MAMMALS, the process of making and transferring pigment to skin cells may be controlled by hormones.

The anterior lobe of the pituitary gland secretes a *growth hormone* controlling body growth, hormones controlling the adrenal and thyroid glands, and three hormones controlling mammalian reproductive functions. The *follicle stimulating hormone,* FSH, stimulates the maturation of eggs in an ovary. The *luteinizing hormone,* LH, causes formation of the *corpus luteum,* a secreting mass of tissue in the ovary. LH together with FSH causes ovulation. *Prolactin* causes milk secretion after pregnancy. J. C. K.

SEE ALSO: DIABETES, ENDOCRINE GLANDS, GIANT, MENSTRUATION, OVARY

Placer Placer is a location where precious minerals are found mixed with gravel and sand. Valuable metals, such as nuggets of gold, tin, platinum, and even diamonds, can be obtained by mining placer deposits.

A placer deposit results from the erosion of rocks containing particles or nuggets of precious metals or minerals. PEGAMITITES and *diamond pipes* are often the source rock for placers. Placer deposits are formed by the concentration of heavy minerals in the sediment of a stream or river. This occurs because these dense minerals are not easily moved and they tend to settle down into the lowest layers of sediment. Placer deposits are found concentrated on the inside of curves where the velocity of the stream is slowest. Placer mining was the principal method employed during the California "gold rush" of 1849, and is still used today. P.P.S.

Plain Plains are large areas of land that are flat or gently rolling. The vegetation usually consists of grass. There are few trees. Plains make up a large part of the earth's surface.

Most *geographers* agree that a plain does not need to have a plane (flat) surface, and that it is not necessarily horizontal or near sea level. The term "plain," however, is used only for those areas where the difference in elevation between the lowest points and the highest points is not more than 500 feet (152.4 meters). Plains, therefore, are no more than gently rolling, and the valleys of plains are shallow.

Over a large area, a plain may rise to a high altitude. An example of a very large inclined plain that rises to a high altitude is the Great Plains region of North America. It gently rises to an elevation of over 5,000 feet (1,524 meters), higher than many plateaus. H.S.G.

Planaria (pluh-NAH-ree-uh) Planaria are freshwater *flatworms.* They have triangular heads and primitive sight organs called eyespots placed so that they seem cross-eyed. The mouth is about in the middle of the body on the underside.

The lateral projections that make up the triangle of the head are called "ears." They are not ears but *olfactory organs.* Eyespots are sunken pigment cups covering a retina.

Outer cells on the body wall have *cilia.* Bodies called *rhabdites* are secreted by the cells. When the rhabdites are discharged, they swell and make a slime sheath around the animal. Muscle fibers run diagonally, around, and up and down in the body wall. There is no body cavity; the space between the wall and internal organs is filled with loosely organized connective tissue cells.

The digestive system consists of a mouth, pharynx, and three-branched intestine. The pharynx lies in a sheath and can be extended out of the body. Bits of food are sucked up into the digestive cavity. Cells lining the cavity engulf and enclose the food in vacuoles where digestion takes place. Food is circulated by the digestive cavity.

Excretion is by ciliated cells called flame cells. These connect to an excretory tube that leads outside the body. Respiration is through the body wall. The nervous system is a ladder type with a "brain" from which four nerve cords extend.

Reproductive systems are complicated and have many parts. Both male and female reproductive organs are in the same animal (MONOECIOUS).

Planaria have the power of regeneration. If cut into three pieces, each piece forms a new worm. Pieces nearest the head regenerate most rapidly because the highest rate of metabolism or functioning is at this end. If pieces are very small, those from the head end may form a head on each end of the piece. Small tailpieces may form two tails. J. C. K.

✳ THINGS TO DO

WILL A WORM GROW TWO HEADS?

1. **Planaria may be purchased from a supply company or may be found in quiet streams and collected in the following way. Put a piece of raw liver in a tall olive bottle. Cover the bottle's mouth with a wire screen to prevent larger animals from getting the food. Tie a cord around the bottle and lower it into the water. The other end may be fastened to a stake driven in the ground on the edge of the bank. It could take several hours before planaria find the liver. Check periodically for signs of a capture.**
2. **Transfer the planaria to a shallow dish of fresh water for its future home. To demonstrate its remarkable powers of regeneration place a planaria on a hard surface. With a sharp razor blade make a cut half way down its anterior end. Place the planaria back in the dish of water.**
3. **It will take about two weeks for each half to grow its other half. As soon as this is apparent feed it raw liver again. Leave the food in for an hour, then remove it to prevent spoilage.**

Plane A plane may be thought of as an endless (infinite) surface that has no thickness. A line that joins any two points in a plane lies entirely in the plane.

SEE ALSO: GEOMETRY

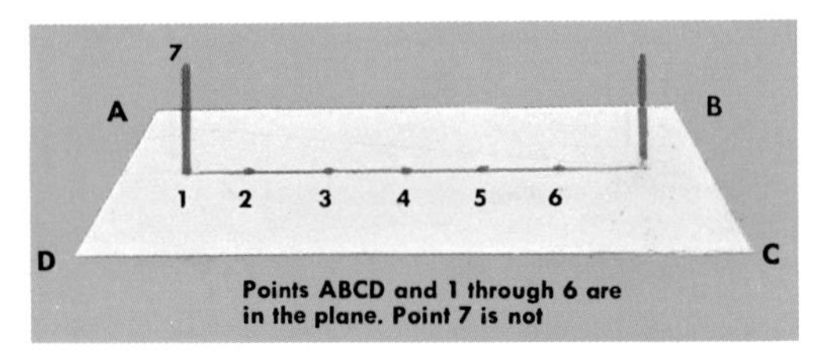

A plane surface

Planet A planet is a body in space that revolves around a star. There are nine planets in the SOLAR SYSTEM, all revolving around the sun. The ancient Greeks were the first to recognize and name some of the planets. The word planet comes from a Greek word meaning "wanderer." The planets appeared to the Greeks to "wander" in the sky.

Planets travel in *orbits* around their stars. All of the planets of the solar system travel in elliptical orbits; that is, their paths are like a flattened circle. The time it takes a planet to travel (revolve) around the sun is called its year. The time it takes a planet to turn (rotate) once on its axis is called its day. All planets revolve around the sun and rotate on their own axes.

Stars shine by self-illuminated light, but we see planets by the light that is reflected off of them from the sun. Even though the planets have no light of their own, they appear very bright because they are much closer to Earth than the other stars.

The Earth and three other planets make up the inner or *terrestrial* planets; the next four planets out from the sun are termed the *giant* planets; the ninth and farthest planet from the sun, Pluto, is in a class by itself.

All of the planets except PLUTO have been explored by spacecraft. MERCURY, JUPITER, SATURN, URANUS, and NEPTUNE have been investigated during a spacecraft flyby. VENUS and MARS have been studied in more detail by soft landings. H.S.G.

SEE ALSO: EARTH, SOLAR SYSTEM

A planetarium projector

Planetarium (plan-uh-TAIR-i-um) A planetarium is a machine inside of a dome-shaped building that can show the sun, the moon, the planets, and the stars. It portrays how all these heavenly bodies move. A planetarium is different from a telescope because a telescope can show a real but very small part of the sky. The planetarium actually makes a large artificial sky appear on its giant domed ceiling.

A planetarium can speed up, slow down, or stop its picture of the sky in action. It can show how the sky looked hundreds of years ago, how it looks now, or how it will look thousands of years in the future. It can show how the sky looks from any place on Earth. A person can sit in Adler Planetarium in Chicago, for instance, and look up at the domed ceiling and see a picture of how the sky looked in Egypt in 2000 B.C. He can see how the sky looks now from the South Pole, or he can see the sky that his great-great-grandchildren will be able to see.

In a very short time, a planetarium can duplicate both the various yearly positions of all of the constellations and the monthly phases of the moon.

Modern planetariums can portray all of the heavenly bodies that are visible to the naked eye. The machine that projects the image of the sky is made up of many projectors, like slide projectors, usually over

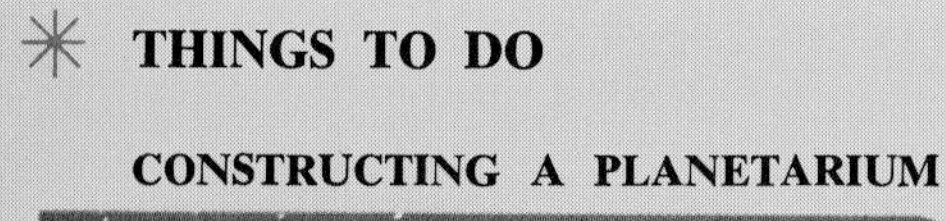

THINGS TO DO

CONSTRUCTING A PLANETARIUM

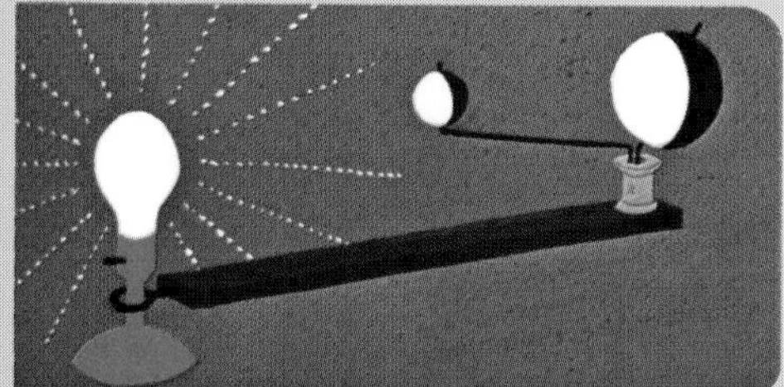

1. **Secure a large rubber ball and a small one which is one-fourth its size. These will represent the earth and moon.**
2. **Insert a wire hanger through the center of both balls. Construct a wooden arm on to a table lamp by following the adjoining illustration. A large eye screw will permit the arm to revolve around the light which represents the sun. A spool nailed to the opposite end of the arm will hold the wires which are attached to the two balls.**
3. **The axis of the earth should always be tilted to the north as you revolve it around the sun. Observe the area on the earth which is directly illuminated by the light at each quarter turn. Can you figure out which season of the year it is? In what positions will the moon be when there are lunar and solar eclipses?**

one hundred. Each projector's picture is a "still" picture. Some are spots of light that represent the sun, the moon, or the planets. Some of them are pictures of groups of stars. The pictures are fitted together to make a single, accurate picture of the night sky. Then, by means of electric motors, the projectors can all be moved to show the individual motions of the heavenly bodies. The complete machine is moved, too, to show the effects of the earth's rotation.

A typical modern planetarium can show over 9600 stars. It has over 100 separate images in each complete sky scene. The first modern planetarium was built in Munich, Germany, in 1923. C. L. K.

SEE ALSO: OBSERVATORY, TELESCOPE

Planetoid see Asteroid

Plankton Plankton includes all the tiny plants and animals that live in both salt and fresh water. Most are microscopic. They are PRODUCERS at the beginning of a food chain—the food for larger life.

Plankton ranges from bacteria and one-celled animals to the larvae of mollusks, worms, and fish. It takes many pounds or kilograms of plankton to produce one ounce (28 grams) of fish. DIATOMS and dinoflagellates (phytoplankton in the Pacific Ocean) provide half the oxygen needed in America. Zooplankton (protozoans, tiny crustaceans, and larvae of larger animals) vary in size from .008 to .9 inch (.2 to 23 millimeters).

Polluted water kills plankton, which cuts off the first link in the aquatic food cycle. Certain biocides, such as DDT, accumulate in algal cells. Even though the water is low in the amount of these pollutants, the algae can store large quantities. Animals that feed upon these plants get concentrated doses. This is called *biological magnification.*

When waste materials cause extreme cloudy or turbid waters, this reduces the light. The phytoplankton cannot carry on PHOTOSYNTHESIS. This happens when industry dumps pollutants. Sewage and other organic wastes in lakes and rivers must be decomposed by bacteria. This consumes large quantities of oxygen and releases carbon dioxide, which upsets the number of other plankton types that can live there. Plankton may soon be on the endangered species list. H.J.C.

SEE ALSO: FOOD CHAIN, MARINE BIOLOGY, OCEANOGRAPHY

Diatoms release oxygen to the atmosphere.

Photomicrograph courtesy of National Teaching Aids, Inc.

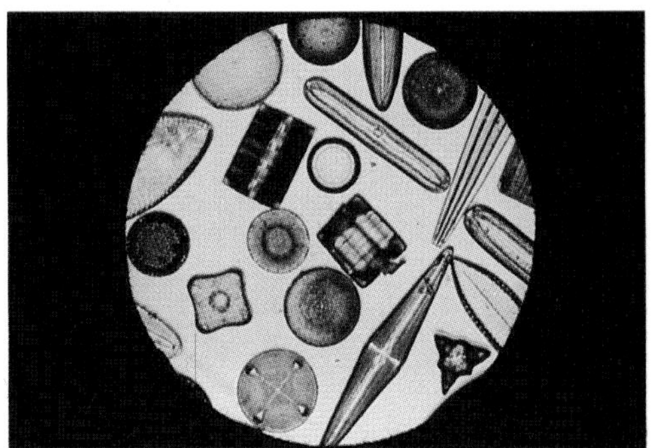

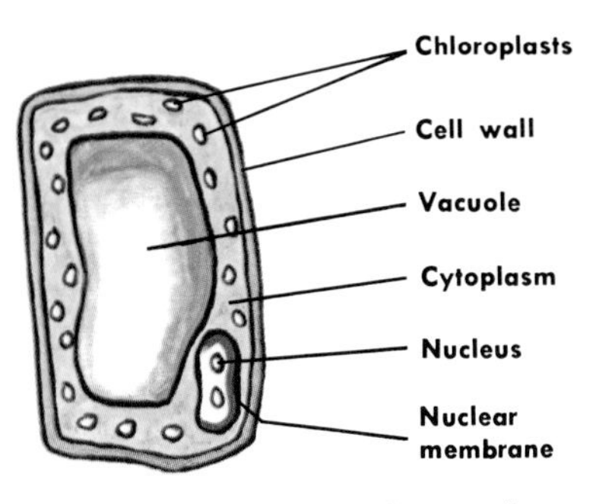

Parts of a typical plant cell

Plant Plants were probably an early form of life that appeared on this earth millions of years ago. They may be so small one cannot see them without a microscope. It would take 5,000 bacteria lined up in a row to measure 1 inch (2.5 centimeters). The largest plants are the giant sequoia trees in California. Some of these are as tall as a twenty-four story building.

Plants are living things that are made of cells, can grow, and reproduce. They carry on most of the same life processes that animals do. They are different from animals in several ways. Most have chlorophyll and can make their own food. In plants of the same kind there is a wide range of size. The higher plants cannot move around from one place to another.

CELLULAR STRUCTURE

All plants are made of cells. The whole plant may be only one cell, such as unicellular ALGAE. Most plants, though, are made up of thousands of cells, with each cell designed to do a certain job for the entire group of cells. Plant cells may be microscopic or as long as 20 inches (51 centimeters).

Most plant cells have a nonliving wall of *cellulose,* a complex carbohydrate. This material makes them more rigid than animal cells. The *cytoplasm* and *nucleus* surround a central *vacuole* of cell sap. A number of bodies are found in the cytoplasm, which are lacking in most animals. *Plastids* help make food, store starch, and contain the colored pigments. The cytoplasm's primary purpose then is to make, store, and digest food.

The nucleus of a cell is the "team captain," controlling most activities carried on in each cell. It contains *chromosomes,* the bearers of hereditary characteristics. Plant cells may have from one to a thousand pairs depending on the species. They usually average from five to fifty pairs. The life span of plant cells varies. Some live only hours while others continue to function for hundreds of years.

METABOLISM

Plants must eat, drink, breathe, and burn up energy. They have one big advantage over animals since most plants make their own food. Plants cannot move and must depend upon the ATMOSPHERE to give them water and fresh air. They use less energy than animals because they do not move from place to place.

METABOLISM is the sum total of all the plant processes necessary to keep it alive. Those activities which build up cells by making complex material from simple materials are termed *anabolism.* Photosynthesis and assimilation are anabolic processes. By contrast, the tearing down of protoplasm, making simple materials from complex materials, is *catabolism.* Digestion and respiration are catabolic processes.

Unicellular plants carry on all life activities within a single cell. This would make this little mass of protoplasm much more generalized than any one cell found in the higher plant groups. Multicellular plants divide up the metabolic responsibilities among the cells. The roots of plants assume the task of anchoring the plant and absorbing the water and minerals from the soil. The stems support the leafy crown and conduct raw materials up to the leaves and, in turn, transport the manufactured food throughout the entire plant. Leaves carry on PHOTOSYNTHESIS, food making, and TRANSPIRATION, release of excess water. The gaseous exchange occurs through minute holes on the leaf.

Materials necessary for metabolism are received and transported in a number of ways. One-celled plants absorb and excrete through the cell wall. Simple multicellular plants pass the material from cell to cell. Higher plants have developed a *vascular* or conducting system. A variety of tubes and vessels are designed to permit a more rapid and continuous flow of raw materials and food products from one part of the plant to another. The *xylem* tissue in the root con-

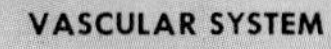

(BLUE) RAW MATERIAL FROM SOIL TRAVELS UP (YELLOW) XYLEM (RED) FOOD TRAVELS DOWN THE (BLUE) PHLOEM

METABOLISM

PLANT BREATHES THROUGH LEAVES—TAKES IN CARBON DIOXIDE AND SUNSHINE

Chlorophyll in the plant makes use of carbon dioxide from air, energy from the sun and raw materials from soil to manufacture food.

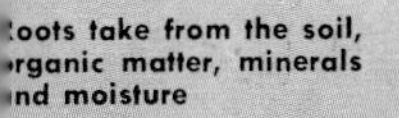

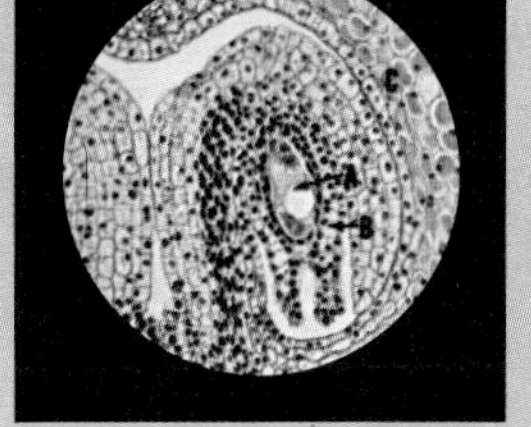

Ovary of a lily plant; A-ovum near funiculus (B), C-ovary wall

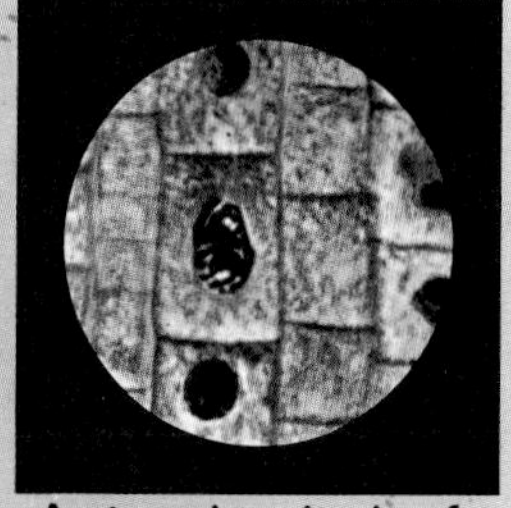

A stage in mitosis of a plant cell, necessary for growth

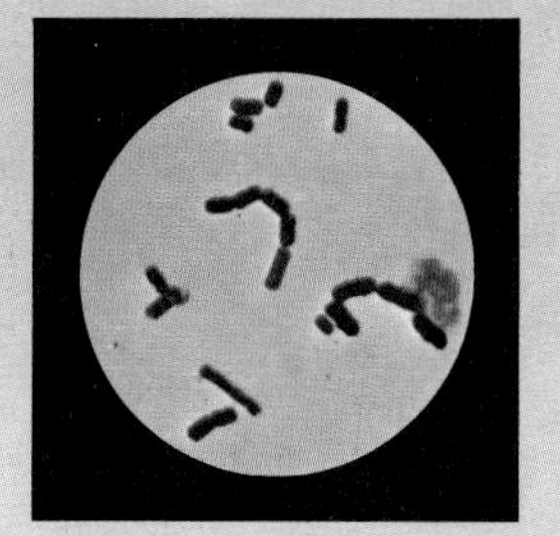

Nitrogen-fixing bacteria that provide nitrates for plants

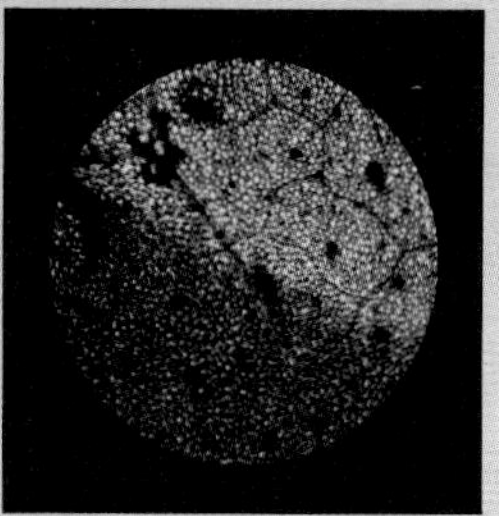

Right half of leaf was covered from sun and could not make starch

Photo-micrographs by National Teaching Aids, Inc.

tinues up the stem, out the *petiole* and through the leaf. *Phloem* tissues form a continuous pathway in the reverse direction, leaves to stems–to roots.

Plants give off oxygen in the process of photosynthesis, and like animals, also release CO_2 in respiration and use O_2 for the oxidation of food. While photosynthesis is taking place during daylight hours, more oxygen than carbon dioxide is released.

GROWTH

Man and other animals do not grow to be giants if they eat and eat. Plants, however, do not stop growing if they are fed and watered more than usual. A geranium growing in Michigan may not get any taller than 2 feet (.6 meter). This same geranium living in a climate where there is a longer growing season, as in California, may be four times taller.

Plants will increase their size in only certain areas. *Meristematic* cells will divide to increase a plant in length and circumference. These four regions are the stem tip, ROOT tip, vascular cambium and cork CAMBIUM. Multiplication of cells occurs more often during the night, because the plant is busy making food during the daylight hours.

Two factors affect the growth in plants. *Genetically* they inherit qualities which affect their size. One can buy seeds to grow giant zinnias or dwarf phlox. Internal cellular activity is another genetic factor. The amount of plant-growth hormone, *auxin,* produced by the cells controls the extent of growth. Finally, the external environmental conditions play a part. Plants given the right amount of water, light, air, warmth and FERTILIZER will thrive better than those deprived of one or more of these.

Most plants will not live forever. There is a certain life span for each kind. ANNUALS will produce seed the first year they are planted. They have completed their life cycle and die. BIENNIALS grow and store food the first year, bloom and produce seeds the second year before they die. PERENNIALS will produce seeds year after year and have a rather indefinite life span. It is reported that some sequoias are 4000 years old.

REPRODUCTION

Plants must make more of their kind or they would soon disappear from the earth. The little one-celled plants just squeeze apart and make two of themselves. Many plants must make two kinds of cells, an egg and a sperm. When these two cells come together the resulting cell will begin to grow into a new plant. New plants usually look like the parent plants.

Plants reproduce asexually by fission, SPORE FORMATION, or by PROPAGATION. Fission is simple division of a cell as in bacteria. If environmental conditions are controlled, bacteria will divide every half hour. This does not appear phenomenal unless one counts the offspring produced in a day and a night. The 48 generations would number 256,000,000,000,000 bacteria.

Spores are cells produced by many plants, such as fungi and one generation of the mosses and ferns. When environmental conditions are adverse, some plants may form spores that have a rather thick wall. This is a protective device of the plant against extreme heat or drought. When conditions are more favorable the spore breaks from the shell and germinates.

Propagation of vegetative parts of a plant (root, stem, or leaves) may be done by the plant itself or by man. Many BULBS will form extra little bulblets. Drooping branches of weeping willows will take root if they come in contact with the ground. Strawberry plants and crab grass send out runners. New shoots and roots arise at the nodes. Man makes leaf, root, and stem cuttings (slips) to propagate the same species.

Plants reproduce sexually by production

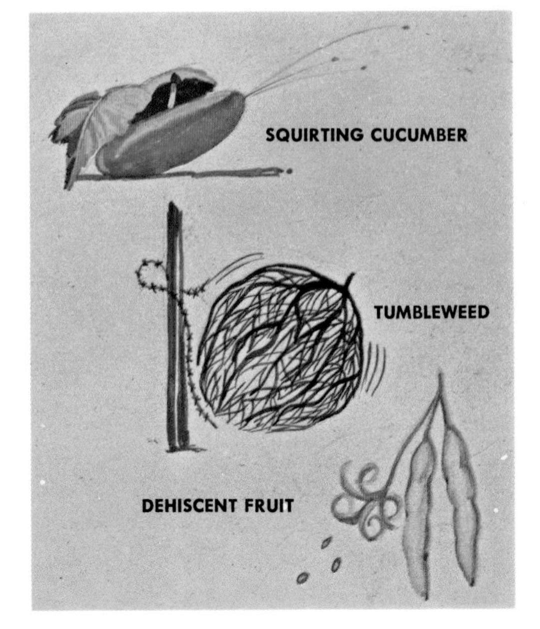

Some unusual types of seed dispersal

of either motile or non-motile sex cells or gametes—eggs and sperm. Conjugation is the union of two sex cells that look alike. Fertilization is the combining of sex cells which can be distinguished as male and female. Sometimes the sexes may be on the same plant as in the apple tree. The ash has male trees (*staminate*) and female trees (*pistillate*).

ADAPTATION

Plants cannot fly south when winter comes as birds do. They are not able to move into the caves or other shelters to hibernate as some animals do when food and warmth are scarce. Since plants cannot move they must adapt to all kinds of conditions. Plants that do not adjust to the environment soon die.

Plants go through seasonal adjustments according to their location. Floral life in California will grow mainly during the wet, cool winters. The hot, dry summers slow growth considerably, almost to inactivity. Many trees lose their leaves during this time. Plants in the frigid zones have adjusted their life activities to a very short growing season as the summers are short and the winters extremely long. In the equatorial rain forests, plants respond by growing almost continually. The forest is very dense and the undergrowth of small plants have adapted to surviving in dense shade.

Another adjustment by plants is the storage of food and water for future use. One

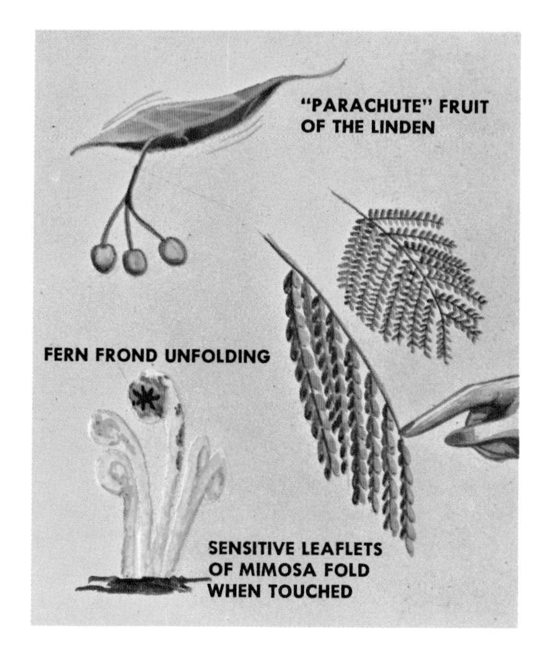

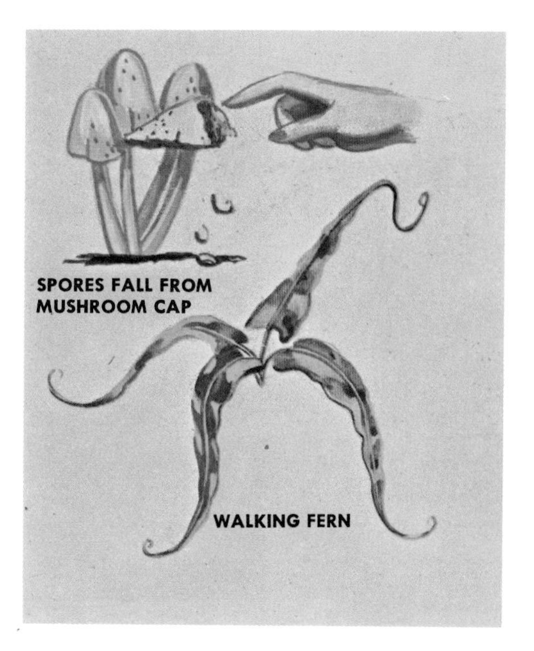

could compare it to animals' preparation for the long winter months. Biennial plants die back to ground level with the roots storing enough material to start the plant on its second year of growth. Some perennials lose their aerial parts when winter arrives and store food in underground stems or roots. Other perennials, such as trees and shrubs, drop their leaves in fall. Roots are unable to absorb water from the frozen ground and must protect themselves from water loss in the leaves.

LOCOMOTION

Most plants do not move from place to place. This is one of the main ways one can tell a plant from an animal. A few of the simple one-celled plants are able to swim or crawl. Nevertheless they are still called plants. Plants are able to bend or turn in different directions. This helps the plant get the things it needs to live.

There are two kinds of movements that stationary plants exhibit. Some movements are due to unequal growth rates in cells and are called TROPISMS. Plants respond in the direction of growth to the direction of the stimulus. If the parts of the plant turn toward the stimulus this is a *positive* response, while moving away is a *negative* response. Stems and leaves turn toward the light but roots grow away from it. Roots grow with the pull of gravity while stems grow up and away from the earth.

Nastic movements are independent of the direction of the stimulus and are characteristically due to changes in *turgor pressure* (water content of the cells) rather than to growth. These are usually temporary or cyclical movements. Flowers open and close periodically. These are called *sleep movements.* If an object touches the leaves of the mimosa plant, they fold up in seconds. When an insect starts to crawl through the Venus' flytrap or sundew the trap folds up, catching the insect inside.

Time-lapse photography reveals the constant motion of plants. Tropic and nastic movements, not always visible to the naked eye, when recorded on film show the plant dancing in tune under the direction of nature's environmental factors. H. J. C.

SEE ALSO: CELL; CELLULOSE; CHLOROPHYLL; HEREDITY; LEAVES; LIFE, CHARACTERISTICS OF; PLANT TISSUES; PLANTS, CLASSIFICATION OF

The roots on these seedlings are growing downward in response to gravity. The stems will grow toward the sun. These are tropisms

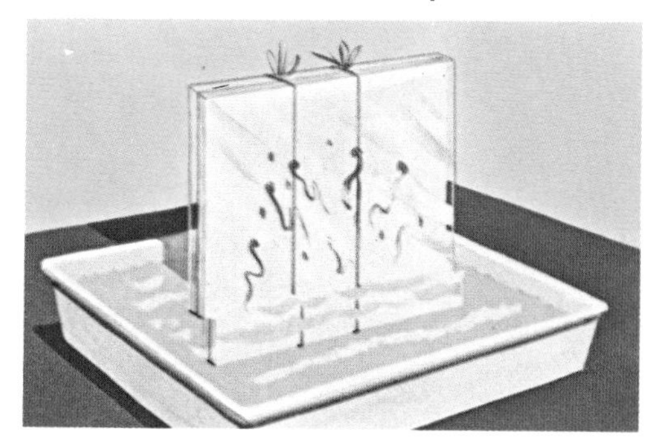

Apple cedar rust spreads from red cedar to apple trees

Plant diseases Plants can become sick just as easily as animals and people. Generally, a disease is any condition that causes a living thing to be unable to function well. Illness can be caused by BACTERIA, FUNGI, or VIRUS. Certain kinds of these organisms live as parasites on other plants; they can destroy healthy tissue. Other organisms cause disease by producing harmful substances (toxins) as waste material.

Plant disorders can also be caused by worms and insects. These animals feed upon plant parts and leave them in such a stripped, unhealthy condition that they may die. Beetles, mealy bugs, aphids, red spiders, scale insects, and mites are a few pests that injure different kinds of plants.

There are times in history when people have starved to death because of serious outbreaks of disease. When the potato crops in Ireland failed in 1845 because of disease, there were many human deaths.

Diseases are carried from one plant to another by wind, water, animals, and man. If seeds, soil, underground stems, and rootstocks are infected, they will spread parasites.

Plant pathologists are scientists who specialize in the study of plant diseases. They are concerned with the life histories of pathogenic organisms (organisms that need to be within a living cell to exist). They must discover what parasites need for growth and reproduction. Only then can they attempt to diagnose methods of control and eradication.

Viruses that attack plants are all pathogenic. Some produce a disease called *chlorosis,* a condition in which the plant can produce little chlorophyll. Other viruses stunt the plant and cause the leaves to yellow and become mottled.

A plant's environment can also cause disease. Too much or too little food (minerals) can make a plant sick. Extremes of temperature, amount of water, and the incorrect degree of acid in the soil are factors affecting healthy growth. Air pollution from industry and transportation do as much damage to plants as to animals and man.

There are many symptoms by which one can detect a "sick" plant. Rapid wilting may occur even though the plant has been well watered. The appearance of tumor-like swellings, scabs, or raised lesions are indications that a foreign matter has invaded the tissues. Other symptoms are the sudden dying of young shoots or leaves, abnormal secretions, or a peculiar odor. Some pests cause spots to form, often brown in color. Dry or wet rotting are other symptoms of sickness. There are many molds and other fungi that are not microorganisms and can be seen on the outside of plants.

Pathogenic bacteria cause such diseases as tomato and cucumber wilt, cotton root rot, fire blight on pears, some galls, and soft rot on various vegetables. Pathogenic fungi cause apple scab, potato blight, wheat rust, corn smut, leaf scorch, and Dutch elm disease.

Other living organisms are also affected indirectly by plant disease. In the food chain, herbivores die without enough plants to eat, and in turn affect humans. People also suffer financially—the annual crop loss in the U.S. due to disease is estimated at 3 billion dollars.

What can be done about this enormous waste of valuable food supply? Prevention or protection against diseases should be the first method of attack. Growers can select seeds and propagating stock that have been treated by application of heat or chemicals. Geneticists are constantly developing seeds that are immune to various diseases. This controlled breeding produces resistant strains. Sterilization of the soil is another technique that can be used by the small plant operator in greenhouses and by home growers. This technique cannot be used by the farmer. He can, however, employ crop rotation. Various kinds of fungi spores need a host each year,

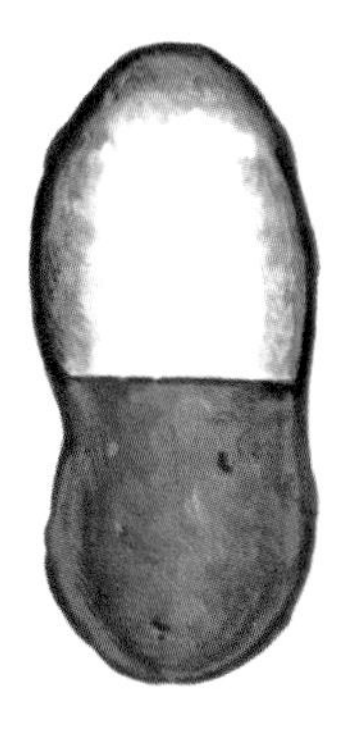

Potato blight is one of the most destructive fungus diseases. The fungus grows on the leaves, and can be spread from plant to plant by wind or splashing of rain

and rotation deprives these pathogens of their food supply.

Quarantine laws set up by state and federal governments keep plant diseases localized. When preventive measures fail and plants become diseased, other methods are available to prevent an epidemic. Fungicides and insecticides can be either sprayed or dusted on plants. Care must be observed in the kind and amount used. Plants can be injured as can be the animals that eat the plants.

Eradication is another method used to control disease. Diseased parts or whole plants are removed and burned. In cases in which a parasite requires two hosts to complete its life cycle, it may be possible to plan to eliminate one host. For example, not growing the common barberry within miles of wheat fields helps to eliminate wheat rust. H. J. C.

SEE ALSO: PARASITE, RUST

Plant hormones see Hormones, plant

Plant pests In addition to the many different kinds of plant diseases, there are a great number of plant pests that can destroy or stop the growth of plants. Insects, especially, carry many of the fungi and bacterial diseases from plant to plant. Bees carry the pear blight even though they do help in the pollination of the trees. The potato beetle carries the potato rot. Boring beetles spread ferment and woodrot fungi.

Insects injure plants when they feed on them. Biting insects such as certain grasshoppers can strip a plant of its foliage, thus killing it. Sucking insects and mites cause damage to plants by reducing their store of plant food, in which case the plant will stop

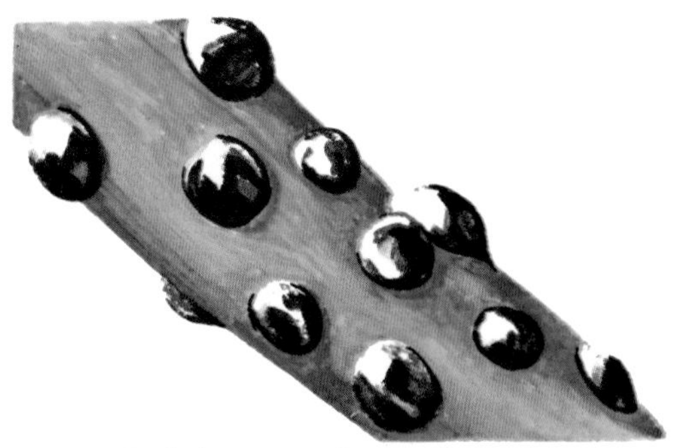

Scale insects suck plant juices.

The boll weevil ruins cotton plant bolls

Courtesy Society For Visual Education, Inc.

Caterpillars damage plants by eating leaves

growing and eventually die. Scale insects, mealy bugs, plant lice, leaf hoppers, and "plant bugs" are the most destructive kinds because they suck the sap out of the plant tissues. Sometimes this only slows up the growth process, but other times it causes irritations by some material the insect may inject into the tissues of the plant. Then the roots or leaves of the plant may develop gall-like swellings. Common injuries of this type are the *Phylloxera* (grape lice) on the leaves and roots of grapes, woolly apple louse on the roots of the apple, and cockscomb gall on the elm.

The growths known as GALLS are also caused by insect larvae developing from eggs

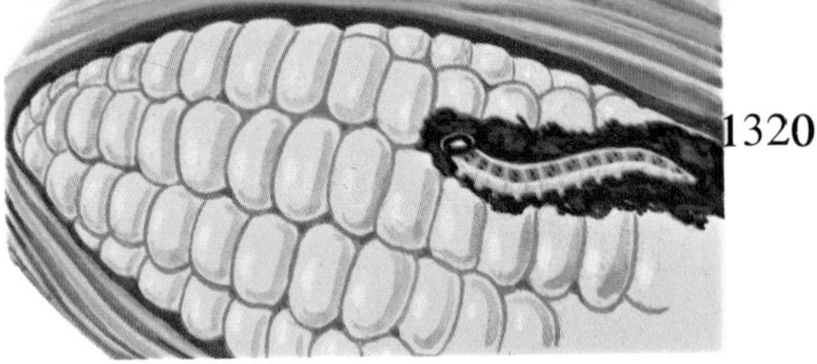

Corn borer

laid in young tissues of a plant. Thousands of plants are attacked by nematode worms which go after the roots and cause gall-like swellings. These worms invade field and truck crops.

Borers injure their host by cutting off the flow of food between the root and leaves of a tree or plant when they bore rings around the trunk or stem. The corn borer is blamed for a great loss of corn crops each year, and this is true; but actually, corn is a favorite food of over 350 other insects. Some of them are the corn-ear worms, chinch bugs, grasshoppers, and the white grubs. The boll weevil does great damage to the cotton crop in the United States each year. It feeds on the silky fiber inside the seed pods or bolls of the cotton plant.

Most birds are friends to the farmers and gardeners because they eat insect pests that are harmful to the crops, but there are some birds that are harmful and are considered plant pests. The crow goes after the farmer's corn crop, and other birds eat or damage fruit in orchards and vineyards. Small animals, mainly in the rodent family, eat grain in the fields and vegetables in the truck gardens. J.K.K.

SEE ALSO: PLANT DISEASES

Plant tissues Most plants are made of many cells. These cells are usually organized into groups called tissues. If a group of cells is basically alike, it is called simple tissue. Complex tissues are made of different kinds of cells which do the same job.

Some tissues appear in all organs of a plant; the stem, root, leaf, fruit, and flower. Other cell groups are so specialized they occur in selected parts of a mature plant. Each kind of tissue has the cellular composition to do a particular function for the life of a plant.

The adjoining table outlines the kinds of cells found in complex plants, their life span, location, and appearance. H. J. C.

SEE ALSO: PLANT

Plants, aquarium see Aquarium, Tropical fish

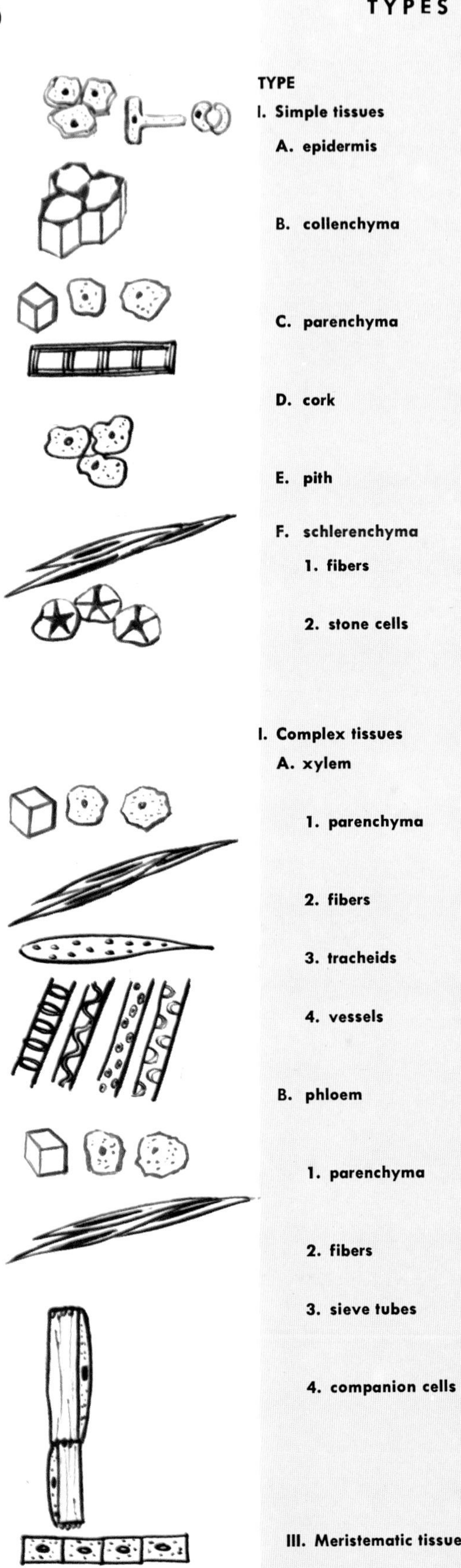

OF TISSUES IN PLANTS

LOCATION	FUNCTION	LIFETIME	APPEARANCE
outer layer of young plants, fruits, leaves of older plants	protective and absorptive	living when functional	irregular shapes may have cutin on outside
many parts of entire plant beneath epidermis of herbaceous stems, petioles, midribs of leaves	strengthening	living at maturity	prism-shaped, elongated, more cellulose in angles of cells
all organs, most common	conduction and storage	usually living	isodiametric, spherical, cubical, many-sided
outer layer of woody plants	water proofing protective	most functional after death	rectangular or box-shaped thick walls of suberin
center core of young plants	food storage	living when functional dies as plant matures	large, thin-walled cells
many parts of entire plant	strengthening	cell contents die at maturity	long, slender, thick-walled
many parts, especially fruit walls		cell contents die at maturity	short, irregular shapes
extend through all parts			
	food storage	usually living	isodiametric
	strengthening	usually dead at maturity	long, slender, thick-walled
	conduction	usually dead at maturity	long, tapering, pitted walls
	conduction	usually dead at maturity	chain of long cells, lack end walls annular, spiral, sclariform, pitted
extend through all parts			
	food storage and conduction	usually living	isodiametric
	strengthening	cell contents die at maturity	long, slender, thick-walled
	conduction	living at maturity	rows of long cells, ends perforated to form a sieve
	helps sieve tubes	living at maturity	long, tapering cells, dense cytoplasm, prominent nucleus
root tip, stem tip — increase length cork cambium, vascular cambium — increase circumference	increases plant growth in length and circumference—cell multiplication	living when functional	rectangular cells

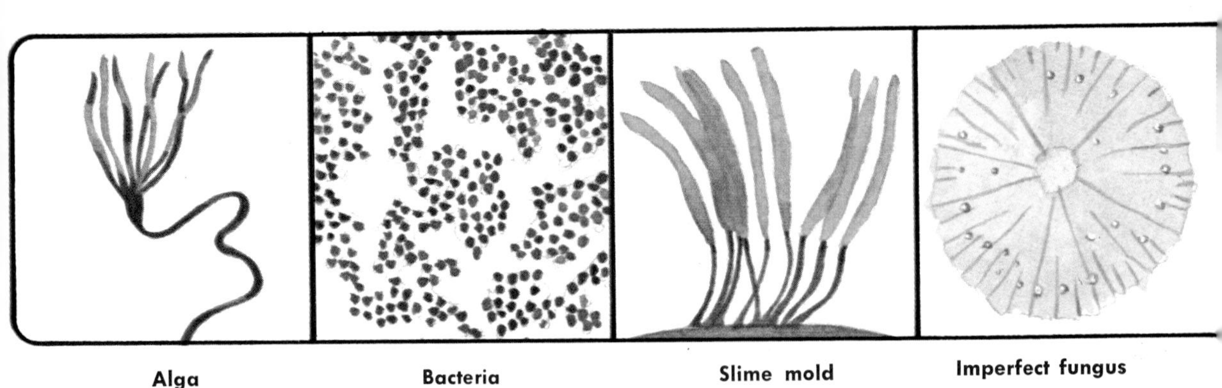

Alga Bacteria Slime mold Imperfect fungus

Plants, classification of While hiking through the United States, one would have difficulty finding a plant that has not been discovered and given a name. The unexplored tropics, though, would prove good hunting grounds for new plants. Every plant that man finds is given two names in Latin or Greek. For example, in France, Australia, or Brazil, *Rosa alba* is a white rose. Over 350,000 plants have been named so far. There are many more to be discovered.

Today plants are classified according to their basic structure and life history. Theophrastus, called *"father of botany,"* was the first scientist to start a classification system, and some of the names he gave plants are still used today. During the Middle Ages man grouped plants according to their uses: medicinal plants, food plants, or harmful plants. This is considered artificial classification. In 1753 CAROLUS LINNAEUS formed a natural classification system based on the number of floral organs. Plants were grouped according to basic similarity of structure.

Plants of relatively like structure and function are classified in the same *species,* related species into a *genus,* genera grouped into *families,* and these into *orders.* Similar orders are placed into *classes,* which are finally classified into *phyla* called divisions.

Taxonomy is a variable science and always is changing because scientists disagree as new plants are discovered.

The earliest FOSSIL plants date back 500 million years to the Cambrian period. *Corallines,* which are algae, were uncovered. This plant life evidently was well established before the first marine animals. It is believed that land plants made their appearance about 350 million years ago. It has been difficult to trace the ancestral progression of existing plants since the soft tissue of many have not left fossil prints. Therefore, there are gaps in the chain of evolution. However, as plants are studied from simple to complex forms, some pattern or thread is found that runs throughout.

ALGAE

The green scum on ponds and the green film that appears in an aquarium is probably some form of algae. They are among the simplest plants that can make food. The entire body of many algae is only one cell. Some cells tend to hang together and form a string or filament. Even when the algae are made of many cells, each cell looks and acts very much like all the others. They do not have roots, stems or leaves.

Algae are put into groups or classified by their color (pigmentation), by the kinds of food they store, and by the kind of cell movement. Algae have one-celled sex organs, or if the organs are multicellular, each cell forms a sex cell. They reproduce asexually by *fission* and by *fragmentation.*

The *blue-green* algae lack an organized *nucleus* and *plastids.* They appear to be the simplest plants within the algae group. The *flagellates* move about and for this reason they are also claimed to be animals by zoologist. The *diatoms* have secreted walls of *silica.* Many move with flagella or an ameboid action. They leave fossil remains. Brown algae are multicellular. The giant KELP of the Northern Hemisphere may be 150 feet (45.7 meters) long. The Sargasso Sea gets its name from a brown alga called *Sargassum.* Red algae are multicellular. They are found at greater depths than any other plant. Irish moss is a red algae.

BACTERIA

Bacteria are often called "microbes" or "germs." They are the smallest living thing

KINGDOM, PLANT

SUBKINGDOM, THALLOPHYTA

- Division, Cyanophyta (blue-green algae)
- Division, Euglenophyta (euglenoids)
- Division, Chlorophyta (green algae)
- Division, Chrysophyta (diatoms, yellow-green and golden-brown algae)
- Division, Phaeophyta (brown algae)
- Division, Rhodophyta (red algae)
- Division, Schizomycophyta (bacteria)
- Division, Myxomycophyta (slime mold)
- Division, Eumycophyta (true fungi)

SUBKINGDOM, EMBRYOPHYTA

- Division, Bryophyta (moss, liverworts)
- Division, Tracheophyta
  - Subdivision, Psilopsida (fossil forms, two living genera)
  - Subdivision, Lycopsida (club moss)
  - Subdivision, Sphenopsida (horsetails)
  - Subdivision, Pteropsida
    - Class, Filicinae (ferns)
    - Class, Gymnospermae (conifer, ginkgo, cycad)
    - Class, Angiospermae (flowering plants)
      - Subclass, Monocotyledoneae
      - Subclass, Dicotyledoneae

in the world. Only a few have CHLOROPHYLL. They grow in three shapes, round, rod-like, or spiral.

Bacteria usually exist as single cells though some form filaments or colonies. They lack a true nucleus and cellulose in their cell walls. Some are able to move by means of projections called *flagella* or *cilia.* Most of these plants are parasitic or saprophytic. A few bacteria can make food and get energy by a process called *chemosynthesis.* It is believed that bacteria are related to the blue-green algae.

SLIME MOLD

This plant creeps along much like the movement of an ameba. It is a slippery, colorless mass of protoplasm. Slime mold is difficult to classify. The reproductive stage is plant-like, while the vegetative stage is animal-like. Therefore, it has received the description of a *fungus-like animal.*

ALGAE
MOSS
LICHEN
DICOT
MONOCOT

GYMNOSPERMS
ANGIOSPERMS
FUNGI
BACTERIA
FERN

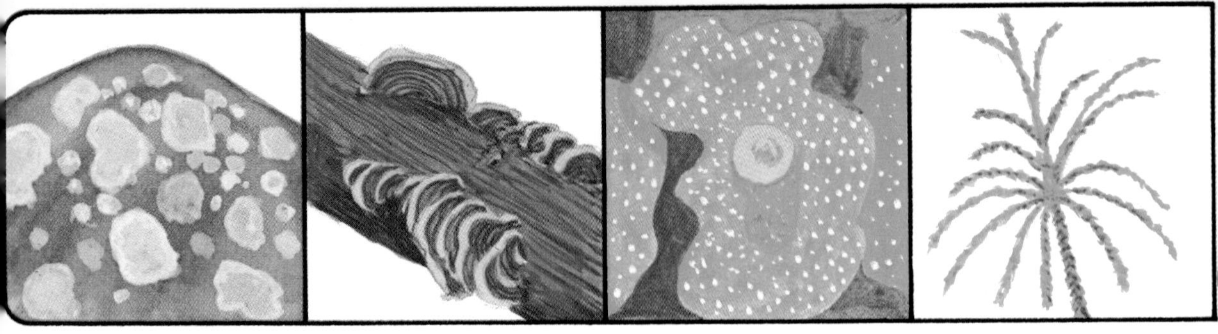

Lichen | Fungus | Moss and liverwort | Club moss

FUNGI IMPERFECTI

The plants in this group are not perfect. They lack the sexual stage in their life cycle. Members of the group include *Penicillium* and other blue-green molds, apple blotch, and a fungus that causes fever and a lung disease in man.

LICHEN

This plant is a combination of plants, a fungus and an alga. The fungus, one of the pair, gathers the water and minerals so the algae can make the food. This living together of two different plants, where one helps the other, is called *symbiosis.*

Lichen grows slowly in patches. It manages to live on trees and rocks. It survives in such bleak areas that it does not have to compete with more vigorous plants.

FUNGI

Some people train their pigs or dogs to find a fungus plant that is good to eat. These plants are called *truffles.* The entire lives of these plants are spent under the ground. They give off strong odors.

The true fungi are the largest group of plants without flowers. They do not have chlorophyll. Many fungi are single-celled, but a *puffball* was found that was 1 foot (.3 meter) high and 4 feet (1.2 meters) wide.

Fungi, with the exception of YEAST, are generally classified according to form and life history instead of function. They lack roots, stems, leaves, and conducting tissue. Usually the plants have two parts: the *vegetative,* consisting of filaments which anchor and absorb; and the *fruiting body,* which does the reproducing.

Fungi usually reproduce by spores. A mushroom will produce as many as two thousand million spores. Some fungi propagate by making a massive ball of *hyphae* (threadlike elements). This ball forms a tough outer coat. Some are as large as footballs and are eaten by Australians who call them "blackfellows' bread".

Many fungi go from one host to another to finish their life cycle; this is called *alternation of hosts.* Wheat rust needs the barberry bush and wheat. The white pine and gooseberry exchange a fungus growth, as do the cedar apple and juniper. The most efficient way to control this alternating fungi pest is to eliminate one of the hosts and halt the cycle.

True fungi include mushrooms, toadstools, tree brackets, smuts, morels, mildews, stinkhorns, ergot, and the beautiful little earthstar.

MOSSES AND LIVERWORTS

These little green plants have parts that begin to look and act like leaves, roots, and stems. Some of the cells in this group are now doing different jobs for the whole plant.

MOSS reproduces by two alternating stages. One shoot of the plant forms eggs while another one makes sperms. Water is needed to carry the sperm to the egg. This fertilized egg germinates, forming a stalk with a capsule on the end. This plant (*sporophyte*) must live on the female plant (*gametophyte*). When the spores are released they will form the male and female plants, thus continuing the cycle.

Different species of moss are grouped according to the position and arrangement of leaves and the shape of the capsule.

CLUB MOSS

Club moss in general appearance resembles true moss but has cones or clubs of spore-bearing leaves. Their life history is similar to ferns but differs in several ways. The spores may not germinate for five years and then do so underground. The *prothallus* grows very slowly, with the sex organs appearing sometimes a dozen years later. After fertilization of the sex cells, a sporophyte germinates. This is the familiar CLUB MOSS.

HORSETAILS

Horsetails are closely related to the ferns, with much the same life cycle. They have underground RHIZOMES as do the ferns.

Horsetail **Fern** **Gymnosperm** **Angiosperm**

They have an erect, jointed shoot instead of compound leaves. There are whorls of little branches around each joint. Cone-like structures produce the spores. Some kinds in tropical America are 30 feet (9.1 meters).

FERNS

These plants have true roots, stems, leaves, and conducting tubes. The LEAVES are compound, meaning many little leaflets on a stem. This makes them more like the flowering plants. Many FERNS have stems underground, with only the leaves *(fronds)* above the soil. A few unusual fern stems have reached a height of 60 feet (18.3 meters) and a width of 2 feet (.6 meter).

There are two plants in a fern's life cycle. The spore germinates into a tiny, heart-shaped *prothallus.* It produces sex cells. Ferns, as mosses, are still dependent upon water for fertilization, to carry the sperm to the egg. The fertilized egg develops into a spore-forming plant (the conspicuous fern plant), which is independent. This is an advance over the *moss cycle.*

GYMNOSPERMS

These plants are woody trees, shrubs, and vines. They are missing the flowers and FRUITS. This is the first group to have seeds. The seeds are not enclosed in a pod, nut, or other organ. Most of them are "evergreen," which means they do not lose their needles or leaves every year. The larches and bald cypresses are exceptions.

Cycads are one of the most primitive seed plants dating back to the Mesozoic Era. They usually have large fern-like leaves, an erect stem, and a tap root. They develop cones in the reproductive cycle.

Ginkgos have thin, fan-shaped leaves that resemble the maiden-hair fern. The sexes are on separate trees. The male tree has drooping *strobili* (cones). The female tree develops a fleshy covering over the seeds which looks like a yellow mottled plum. This is not classified as a true fruit.

The conifers (cone-bearers) include the pine, hemlock, spruce, fir, juniper, and many others. Most of them bear both sexes on the same tree but in different catkins. They produce two kinds of spores. The pollen grain is the male gametophyte, while the ovule is the female. The union causes the embryo development which, when mature, is the seed.

ANGIOSPERMS

Any plant with a flower belongs in this group. Man has discovered and named more ANGIOSPERMS than all the lower plants put together. They are the most complex and most recent plants in the world. They are adapted to living in a wider range of places than any other single group.

Flowers may be large and conspicuous or small and less striking. Most angiosperms have the STAMEN and PISTIL on the same plant and frequently in the same flower. A flower is *complete* when it has all floral parts, *incomplete* when one or more is missing. A perfect flower has both stamen and pistil, while an imperfect has only one, as in the willow, poplar, and mulberry trees. Only in the flowering plants is there double fertilization. One sperm in the POLLEN grain unites with the ovum in the ovary to form the embryo. The other sperm joins the polar nuclei to form the *endosperm.* This feeds the embryo.

Angiosperms are separated into two groups. *Monocotyledons* have one *cotyledon,* leaves with parallel venation, flower parts in multiples of three, vascular bundles in the stem, no cambium, and include such plants as grasses, lilies, and orchids.

Dicotyledons have two cotyledons, leaves with netted venation, flower parts in multiples of four or five, vascular bundles in a ring, a cambium for secondary growth, and include such plants as legumes, roses, mint, and most forest and fruit trees. H. J. C.

SEE ALSO: ALTERNATION OF GENERATIONS; EMBRYOPHYTA; EVOLUTION; GEOLOGIC TIME TABLE; PLANT; PLANT TISSUES; REPRODUCTION, ASEXUAL; REPRODUCTION, SEXUAL; THALLOPHYTA

Courtesy Society For Visual Education, Inc.

Leaves of Venus' flytrap close on insects

Plants, insectivorous (in-seck-TIHV-uh-ruhs) Some herbs have special leaves that trap small animals and insects. They secrete a protein-digesting ENZYME. Protein is only a supplemental source of food. All insect-eating plants also carry on PHOTOSYNTHESIS. Most of these plants are small. They are found in swamps or bogs, or in dry, rocky places. They often live in bogs and have a limited root system.

The PITCHER PLANT has a trumpet or pitcher that may be 8 inches (20.3 centimeters) long and 3 inches (7.6 centimeters) across. It is red or green streaked with yellow and purple. Inside the pitcher, hairs pointing downward lead insects to the honey glands. The plant has a single, perfect FLOWER and a capsule fruit. It is in the family Sarraceniaceae.

The SUNDEW, the most highly developed of all the insectivorous plants, has a basal rosette of round leaves. It possesses tentacle-like stalks with sticky end glands. Insects touching these are trapped as the leaf folds over. Flowers form an inflorescence which matures into a capsule fruit. The sundew is in the family Droseraceae.

The VENUS'-FLYTRAP has leaves with two halves. Stiff bristles or hairs with glands appear on the upper surface. When an object touches the hairs, the leaf closes up like a book. This plant is also in the family Droseraceae.

Bladderwort, an aquatic herb, has leaves that float on the surface. Small valvelike openings trap tiny water insects. This herb is in the family Lentibulariaceae. H. J. C.

Plants, medicinal Since ancient times when man first gathered the seeds, stems, leaves, and roots of plants, he has tried to use them to cure illnesses. Early man would boil, dry, or powder the plants to make herb medicines.

In modern times, medical scientists have found that some of these plants proved useful, while others either needed much refining or were useless, or perhaps even harmful.

One of the old plant medicines scientifically proved valuable is QUININE. When the Spanish explorers came to Peru in the sixteenth century, South American Indians were using cinchona tree bark with its quinine to treat "swamp fever." Quinine is still one of the best drugs for malaria.

Two long known beverage plants, coffee and tea, provide the useful drug CAFFEINE ($C_8H_{10}N_4O_2$). Caffeine is extracted from the beans of the coffee plant. Its pure white crystals are prescribed by doctors as a stimulant to nerve activity. Often caffeine is mixed with aspirin and sedatives used for colds because it offsets their depressing action on heart and brain.

Certain plants of the nightshade-potato family (*Solanaceae*) give man two medicines: *atropine* and *belladonna*. These will slow the secretion of certain glands and will relax over-tense intestinal muscles. Atropine will enlarge the eye pupils so that the doctor can examine one's eyes.

People of old China, as in other old cultures, used many herbs now shown to be useless. But the ancient Chinese did use plants of the *Ephedra* group which act like the modern animal gland extract ADRENALIN. The plant they called *ma huang* (*Ephedra equisetina*) has the chemical *ephedrine* which helps people who have asthma.

The shiny-leaved, tiny wintergreen of the north woods has a medical use in addition to its value in flavoring. Wintergreen oil is

Some plants used to obtain medicines: (from left) coffee, cinchona, poppy

prescribed as a liniment rub for sore muscles. A cheap grade of liniment is now made from camphor (tree) extract.

Several medicines for heart diseases come from long known herbs. *Digitalis purpurea,* the common garden FOXGLOVE, was used by early peoples of Africa and the East Indies. Careful doses of digitalis extract speed up a weak, slow heart. By contrast, the drug *aconite* from leaves of monkshood will slow down the heart when it beats too fast, as during high fever.

All parts of castor oil plants, grown as garden oddities, contain both the poison *ricin* and also (in the castor beans) the skin lubricant and laxative, castor oil.

The two most widely grown narcotic-yielding plants are the Asian OPIUM poppy and the South American coca tree. The coca tree (*Erythroxylon coca*) is not to be confused with cacao trees (chocolate, cocoa) nor with cola trees (cola beverage). Poppy seed pods yield crude *opium* and *morphine;* coca leaves give *cocaine*. All NARCOTICS are dangerously habit-forming but are valuable in small, brief doses for severe pain.

Many other plants contain chemicals used in medicines. These include: juice of grapes, sugar cane, and beets (fermented to make medicinal alcohol); *henbane* and Jimson weed (drugs similar to belladonna); *cascara* leaves (laxatives); tanbark oak (tannic acid for skin burns); and several mint family plants (Menthol, peppermint, etc. for tonics). D.A.B.

SEE ALSO: DRUGS, PHARMACOLOGY

Plants, succulent Some plants have the capacity to store up large amounts of water. These kinds of fleshy plants are succulents. Most live in dry, desert-like conditions. They are able to survive because they can maintain a balance between water output and input. Leaves on succulent plants may be small or absent. Spines or thorns often develop. When leaves are present, they are usually thick and fleshy. Stems grow in many shapes and forms.

Many of the succulent plants have large, brightly colored flowers. Often the root systems are shallow, an adaptation to absorb what little rain that does fall. Succulent plants cannot stand frost or frequent rains.

Macmillan Science Company

Many desert plants are succulents

Ecologically these plants are classified as *zerophytes* since they can exist upon a limited amount of water. The openings (stomata) on the leaves are depressed in tiny pockets. This cuts down on the rate of TRANSPIRATION. The epidermis of zerophytes is covered with a thick, waxy layer or cuticle. Some species, during extreme drought, have so little water that most cellular activity is dormant. Others drop their leaves during dry spells. Still others only open their stomata during the night. Many succulents have more than the usual number of fibers and stone cells (sclerenchyma cells). These keep the plants strong and stiff and prevent wilting when the water supply is short.

The CACTUS, YUCCA, AGAVE, SEDUM, stonecrop, hen and chickens, and JOSHUA trees are all succulents in various families of plants. H. J. C.

Plants, tropical Plants that grew originally in the regions near the equator are called *tropical* plants. They grow in deserts, on mountains, in jungles, grasslands, swamps, and forests. Tropical plants are common in the East and West Indies, Central and South America, Malaya, parts of Africa and Australia, and India. Tropical countries have a wet season and a dry season. Because there is no winter season, tropical plants grow during the entire year and grow large, dense, and in great variety. Many tropical plants are evergreen; others shed their leaves during the dry season, but new growth starts immediately.

EXPORT PLANT PRODUCTS

Man depends on tropical plants for many food products, medicines, clothing, and

Buchsbaum
The passion flower of tropical America

building materials. Pineapples, bananas, dates, coffee, bamboo, cocoa, tea, sugar, nuts, hemp, quinine, avocados, citrus fruits, cotton, coconuts, melons, beans, and hardwoods come from tropical plants.

Some tropical plants such as dieffenbachia, poinsettias, begonias, and cacti are raised as house plants in cold climates. Palms, rhododendrons, orchids, and ferns are often found in greenhouses and conservatories.

TROPICAL PLANTS IN THE GARDEN

Many common garden plants which originated in the tropics have been adapted to temperate climates. *Cleome,* or SPIDER PLANT, has claw-like pink and white clusters of flowers that give the plant a spidery appearance. *Bleeding-heart* has red and white tubelike flowers that resemble small hearts. *Clematis* is a tropical vine that likes rich, moist soil and has many pink, purple, blue, white or yellow blossoms. *Lantana* shrubs are tropical plants with dense clusters of tiny flowers. The *oleander* has large clusters of red, pink, white, or purple flowers. The *canna* has bright, showy leaves and flowers. *Water lilies* and *lotus* plants have thick, fleshy stems, with air pockets that enable leaves and flowers to float. Most bloom during the day, but the Egyptian white lotus is an exotic night-blooming plant. The beautiful blue *Nympaea* lotus was revered by ancient Egyptians. The Hindus consider the Indian lotus a sacred plant. The largest water lilies, *Victoria Cruzianas,* are sturdy enough to support a small child.

TROPICAL FOOD PLANTS

There are many tropical food plants that are so perishable, difficult to transport, or costly to market that they are seldom seen outside of the tropics. These foods are often mentioned in stories, poems, and songs. The tropical MANGO tree is well known for its delicious fruit. Its leathery leaves on wide spreading branches make mangoes valuable as shade trees as well as fruit trees. Mango fruit is rich, sweet and spicy tasting. The oval, large, red-orange fruit is rich in vitamin A and C. *Breadfruit, jackfruit,* and *durian* are tropical fruits with rough spiny outer coverings. Breadfruit resembles a muskmelon. When cooked, it tastes something like a sweet potato. Jackfruit is a giant fruit that is sometimes 2 feet (.6 meter) long, and weighs up to 40 pounds (18 kilograms). Durian is a fruit with a characteristic strong odor. PAPAYA is a juicy melon-like fruit. This yellow fruit grows directly out of the tree trunk. The *soursop* is an evergreen tree bearing oval-shaped, green fruit. The tart, juicy flesh of the fruit is used in beverages and sherbets. The *sweetsop* is a deciduous tree. Its cone-shaped, 8-inch (20.3-centimeter) long fruit tastes like sweet custard. The *passion* fruit grows on a vine called *passiflora.* The *passion flower* of tropical America is purple and white and about 3 inches (7.6 centimeters) wide. The markings of the flower resemble the cross used in the Crucifixion. This gives the plant its name. Natives of the tropics chew the *Betel* palm fruit. Their teeth are stained by the red fruit, but it is considered an aid to digestion. Roots of the *cassava* are eaten as starch vegetables or ground into flour. *Tapioca* comes from cassava. *Yams* are roots from a vine. Sometimes these roots weigh more than 40 pounds (18 kilograms). YAMS are prepared like potatoes.

SOME ORNAMENTAL PLANTS

A beautiful tropical flower is the *bird of paradise.* Its tall thin stalk and orange and blue flower head resemble a bird's neck and head. Stiff leaves, 3 to 4 feet (.9 to 1.2 meters) long, are at the base of the plant. *Bougainvilleas* are vines belonging to the four-o-clock family. Their colorful modified leaves enclose small flowers. This adds to the size of the blossoms. Flowers are shades of purple, red, or gold, and bloom in long, waving sprays. The *wooden rose* vine

Phyllis Neulist

1—UMBRELLA PALM
2—BOUGANVILLEA
3—BANANA (FLOWER)
4—HIBISCUS
5—BREADFRUIT
6—ACACIA TREE
7—TREE FERN

Buchsbaum

Phyllis Neulist

Buchsbaum

grows like a morning-glory. The dried seed pods it produces look like a rose carved from wood. These seed pods are used in dried flower arrangements. The *climbing pothos* vine is raised for its beautiful shiny leaves, that are sometimes 2 feet (.6 meter) long. Air slots appear in the sides of the larger leaves, allowing wind to pass through the vine without damage. This vine grows on palm trees for support. Its weight often kills the tree. *Frangipani* or *temple* tree is a deciduous tree about 35 feet (10.7 meters) tall. The tree flowers before the leaves appear and continuously thereafter. Fragrant yellow, white, or red clusters of flowers are at the ends of the stiff, blunt branches. Frangipani flowers are used in making Hawaiian leis. In Ceylon and India these trees are planted in temple gardens. The *African tulip* tree or *Spathodea,* is a 50 foot (15.2 meter), evergreen tree. Throughout the year red flowers, shaped like cups, bloom on the ends of the high branches. The *traveler's tree* has leaves that resemble banana tree leaves. They are arranged like parts of a giant fan, up to 40 feet (12.2 meters) tall. Rain water collects at the base of the leaf stalks, and water can be obtained by cutting into these stalks. The EUCALYPTUS is sometimes called the *stringy-bark* or *gum* tree. These evergreen trees grow rapidly up to 300 feet (91.4 meters) tall. *Acacias* are shrubs or trees. Their flowers are yellow or white and grow in fluffy clusters. The national flower of Australia is the *wattle,* an acacia.

OTHER UNUSUAL PLANTS

Giant flowers are found among *Rafflesia* plants. The tubers of this plant weigh over 100 pounds (45.3 kilograms). The plant is a PARASITE which attaches itself to ground vines. The flowers may be 3 feet (.9 meter) wide and as tall as a man. They give off an unpleasant odor to attract carrion flies. *Krubi* is a giant flower that grows up to 8 feet (2.4 meters) tall and has a disagreeable odor. *Mangrove* trees grow in salt water swamps and support themselves with prop roots. These roots grow down from the trunk and branches. Many of the wild FIG and EBONY trees produce fruit and flowers on their trunks and branches.

The tree fern is a true fern that grows to 60 feet (18.3 meters) tall. It is similar to coal age ferns and thus is termed a "living fossil." M.R.L.

SEE ALSO: GEOLOGIC TIME TABLE

Plasma (PLAZ-mah) Plasma is the fourth state of matter. A plasma is produced when matter is heated to a temperature, at which point atoms give up some or all of their electrons.

Plasmas are often used in lighting systems. Mercury vapor, at low pressure, is in fluorescent lamps. The mercury is ionized by a current at each end of the tube. It conducts a current that causes the vapor to radiate. This radiation makes phosphorous coating on the tube glow. A.J.H.

Plasma see Blood

Plasma membrane see Cell

Plaster Plaster is a hard material that is coated on walls and ceilings inside buildings. Plaster comes as a powder of cementing chemicals and fine sand.

Different plaster powders contain various amounts of unslaked lime, GYPSUM, and Portland cement. Hair or fibers are also included in the powder mix in order to give strength to the finished plaster coat.

When a plastering job is started the dry plaster powder and sand are mixed with water. The thick, creamy mixture is quickly applied to the *lath* or other plaster base. Plaster bases are the rough surfaces of walls and ceilings. They may be made of concrete blocks, hollow tile, brick, gypsum board or lath. Lath consists of strips of wood or steel having air spaces between strips. The soft, fresh plaster works into such spaces and thus helps keep the dried plaster clinging to the surface.

When mixes of plaster are used for outdoor wall coatings, they are called *stucco.* For smoothly finished, indoor surfaces, a second coat of fine, sandless lime plaster is put onto the first, or rough, undercoat.

Plasterboard is machine-made wall covering. It consists of pairs of sheets of heavy paper or fiberboard containing a sandwich-like filling of gypsum plaster. D. A. B.

SEE ALSO: CEMENT

Plaster of Paris When gypsum is heated over 120° C. (248° F.), it loses water and becomes the white powder, plaster of Paris $(CaSO_4)\ 2H_2O$. When water is added to the powder, it hardens into a solid mass; so plaster of Paris is used for plasters, models, and molds.

SEE ALSO: GYPSUM

Plastic surgery Plastic surgery is a specialized form of medical surgery. It generally deals with the reconstruction of external body tissue that has been damaged or is deformed. Its goal is to improve the function and/or the appearance of body parts.

Plastic surgery is often conducted on the most visible areas of the human anatomy, especially the face. Some common operations are for cosmetic purposes. Reshaping the nose is called *rhinoplasty,* while reducing protruding ears is termed *otoplasty.* Various types of "face-lifts" tighten the skin to remove wrinkles. *Lipectomy* removes fat cells from specific body areas. The use of silicon inserts to enlarge breasts in females was restricted in the U.S. in 1992.

Some types of plastic surgery serve important medical needs. *Skin grafting* is often used to replace dead skin that has been destroyed by burns with living tissue. Severe injuries of the hand often require the transplantation of bones, nerves, tendons, and skin to restore some degree of usefulness. Organs and tissues needed for such operations may come from the patient or from a compatible donor. J.H.

SEE ALSO: SURGERY, TRANSPLANT (ORGAN)

Plastics Plastics are a large group of synthetic materials made by chemists. Plastics are made of MOLECULES formed by CARBON atoms and one or more additional ELEMENTS, such as hydrogen, oxygen, nitrogen, fluorine, chlorine, and a few others. These elements form especially long molecules that have different properties based on their structures. Under certain conditions, plastics can be molded into many useful shapes, including handles, toys, dishes, even parts of automobiles and airplanes.

Plastics are either *thermoplastic* or *thermosetting.* Celluloid, which was invented in 1856

Structure and uses of one basic plastic chemical, butadiene with formula C_4H_6

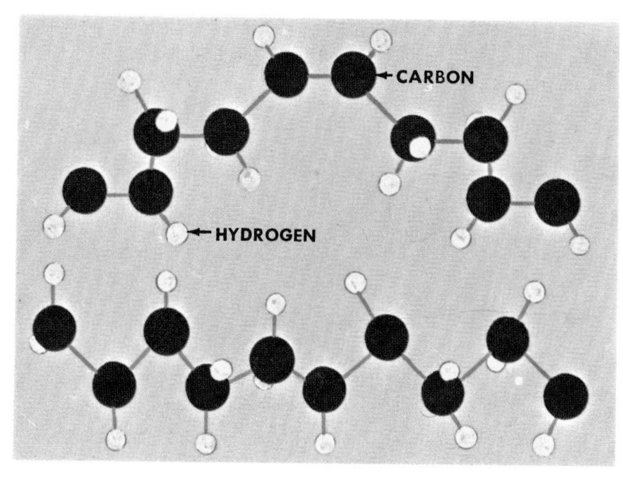

Polybutadienes, or butadiene plastic polymers: the molecules can join together, or polymerize, in different ways. The plastic in the upper figure is rubbery; the lower one is fibrous

Rohm and Haas photo

The Climatron at the Missouri Botanical Garden has a roof, or protective "skin," of acrylic plastic

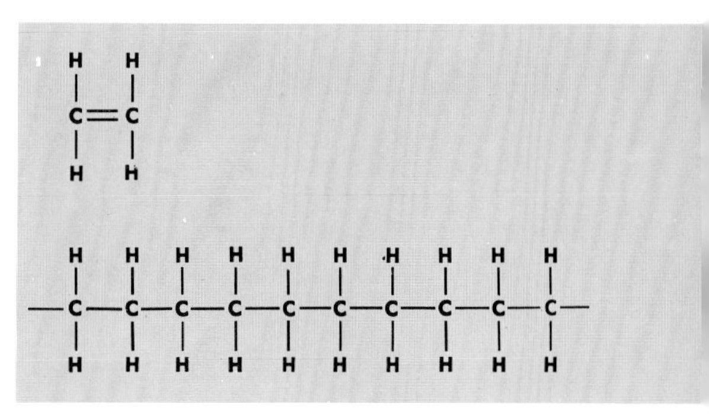

In this example of polymerization (right), the original molecule is ethylene, a gas. The linear chain is a polyethylene plastic

by Alexander Parkes, is thermoplastic; it can be softened again and again by high temperatures and remolded. Bakelite, discovered by Leo H. Baekeland about 1910, is thermosetting; once formed, it cannot be melted and reshaped. Heating does not change the atomic order or chemical structure of thermoplastic materials. The molecular weight and chemical structure of thermosetting plastics, however, are changed by heating.

Plasticizers, high-boiling-point liquids, are used in paints and in thermoplastics. These materials make the plastic pliable at lower temperatures and improve such properties as water resistance, firmness, and flexibility in the final product.

POLYMERIZATION

Many plastics are formed by polymerizing simpler chemicals, usually gases or liquids. *Polymerization* means the joining together of small molecules into larger ones under the influence of heat and a catalyst. When *ethylene,* as a liquid, is heated under very high pressure with small amounts of oxygen, many molecules combine to form the plastic *polyethylene.* Polyethylene is a tough solid which has valuable insulating properties and is resistant to most chemical solvents. It is used as a protective coating and for making containers. Based on the length of its molecular chains, polyethylene (and other plastics) can be given many different qualities.

Similar molecules, called *vinyls,* are also polymerized to become plastics used in garden hoses, insulating materials, and the transparent trade product, *Saran.* A newer type of plastic, called *Teflon,* exhibits the qualities of thermosetting. Its molecular chains are three-dimensional, often referred to as *cross-linked,* and are not softened by heat.

PHENOLIC OR FORMALDEHYDE RESINS

Resins, organic substances from certain plants, are among the earliest synthetic plastics and were studied by Leo Baekeland. The terms "resin" and "plastic" are sometimes used interchangeably. In more careful use, resin refers to the polymer, and plastic to the product obtained from the resin by incorporating plasticizers, fillers, and dyes.

Continuous heating of a phenolic resin creates larger and larger chains. The polymerized product becomes firmer and firmer. As the molecular weight increases, the activity eventually decreases so that there is a practical limit to the size of a polymer molecule.

GLYPTALS

Polymers prepared from *glycerol* and *phthalic* acid are known as *glyptals.* They have cross-linking, which makes them useful in synthetic enamels for finishes on automobiles and kitchen appliances.

FOAMED PLASTICS

These materials, which are porous and of low density, are valuable for insulation, cushioning, and packaging materials, among other uses. They can be made by dispersing a gas evenly through a resin before it is set. The gas expands as the resin sets, creating pores in the finished materials. Because some foamed plastics such as *styrofoam* and *urethane* may contain gases harmful to the environment, their use in some applications became controversial during the early 1990s.

COMPOSITE PLASTICS

By reinforcing various plastics with strands of glass or other materials, plastic can be made as strong as many metals. The fibers may be arranged in one direction, or at right angles, or in all directions, depending on the kind of reinforcement that is needed. J.R.S./J.H.

SEE ALSO: ORGANIC COMPOUNDS, RESIN, SYNTHETIC FABRICS

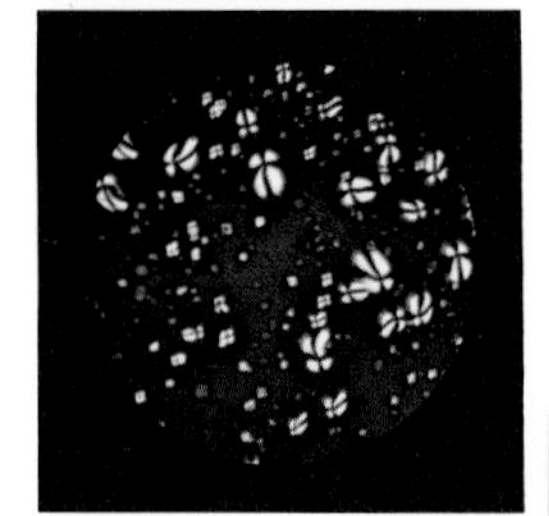

Cell of potato tuber. Leucoplasts enclose the developing starch

Photo-micrographs by National Teaching Aids, Inc.

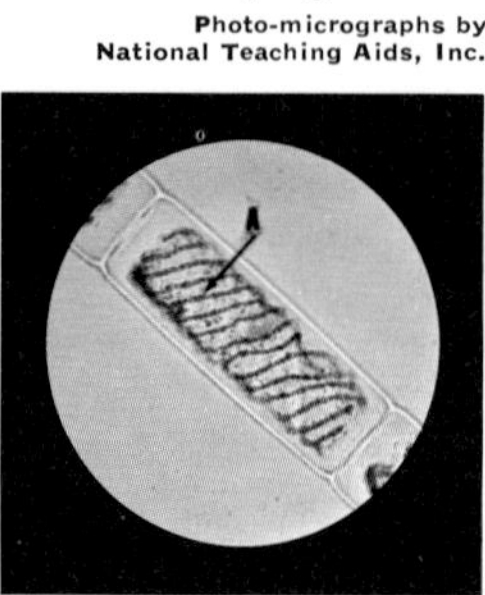

Spirogyra, a green alga. "A" is the chloroplast

Photo-micrographs by National Teaching Aids, Inc.

Plastid (PLASS-tidd) There are small bodies in plant cells that are made of colored material. They are named *plastids.* The CHLOROPHYLL in plastids makes the leaves green. A carrot has orange plastids, and a beet has red ones. The plastids in a white potato have no color. The plastids help a plant to make food or to store it for use later.

Plastids are formed from the cytoplasm in the cell or from the division of other plastids. Usually plastids have a definite shape and are the center of a special chemical action. *Chloroplastids* (*chloros*—green) make carbohydrates from carbon dioxide, water, and light—the process of PHOTOSYNTHESIS. Chlorophyll is always contained in plastids, except in blue-green algae and photosynthetic bacteria. *Chromoplastids* (*chromos*—color) may contain two chemicals—XANTHOPHYLL and carotenes—which give the yellow color to many fruits, vegetables, and autumn leaves. *Leucoplastids* are colorless and contain starch. H. J. C.

Plate tectonics Plate tectonics is the area of GEOLOGY that deals with the nature of movement in the EARTH's crust. It combines the theories of CONTINENTAL DRIFT and seafloor spreading to explain the present-day locations of the continents and the oceans.

The theory of plate tectonics deals with the concept that the earth's crust is divided into nine major and several minor plates. It suggests that these plates are capable of movement, and are continually being rejuvenated by new material brought up from the *mantle.* As new material is added

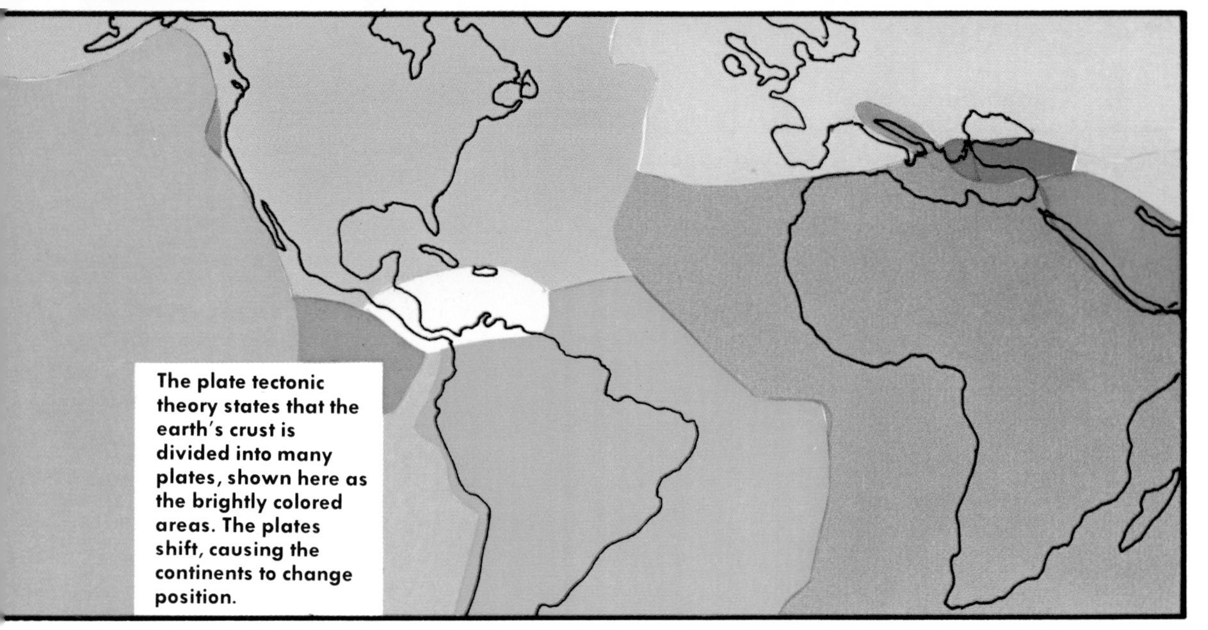
The plate tectonic theory states that the earth's crust is divided into many plates, shown here as the brightly colored areas. The plates shift, causing the continents to change position.

to the plates by a *submarine ridge* system, older sections of crust are sinking back down into the mantle at a *trench* and are being remelted. The continents, which sit on top of most plates, appear to be drifting apart from each other, but, in reality, it is the movement of the plates themselves that is responsible for this apparent motion.

Motion in the crustal plates begins at the submarine ridges where molten material is pushing upward from the mantle and spreads apart the existing sections of crust. This movement will continue until a continent is carried as far as a trench, or until two large continents collide and are welded together. Most of the major mountain systems have their origin in the collision of continents, or are a result of plate movement.

Geological evidence indicates that the last major episode of plate tectonics began about 200,000,000 years ago, and it continues today. Geological evidence of other episodes is scant. Current evidence indicates that the present distribution of continents will certainly change in the future.

P.P.S.

Plateau (platt-TOH) A plateau is an elevated flat area. Plateaus may be a few hundred feet high or thousands of feet high. In most cases they are distinctly above the surrounding lands, but some are flat lands surrounded by mountains.

Some plateaus are small, but most are hundreds of square miles in area.

Plateaus developed from upheavals of the earth's surface when mountains were being formed from lava flows and from settling of the surface which left one portion higher. Most plateaus are worn and gullied away, giving the appearance of being a mountain region. A dramatic example of EROSION at work on a plateau is the Grand Canyon, formed in the Colorado Plateau of the West. The greatest plateau, however, is found in Tibet.

D. J. I.

SEE ALSO: GEOLOGY, MESA, NORTH AMERICA

Platelets see Blood, Circulatory system

Platinum (PLATT-ih-nuhm) Platinum is a grayish-white metallic element. It is more precious than gold. Platinum was discovered in the 15th century by an Italian chemist. It is usually found in ores with other related elements, but some pure platinum occurs. Pure and compound ores are found mainly in the Ural Mountains of Russia; Colombia, South America; Canada; and the Pacific Coast of the United States.

Platinum is heavy and malleable. It can be drawn into a fine wire and hammered into thin sheets. It does not oxidize in air, which means that it will not tarnish. It is resistant to heat and most chemical reagents but will dissolve in aqua regia. It is corroded by chlorine, sulfur and caustic alkalies. It combines readily with most metals. Platinum melts about 1770° C. (3218° F.), making it useful in high-melting-point alloys.

Plantinum is easily welded and therefore

is valuable in the manufacture of delicate laboratory and surgical instruments and various electrical apparatus.

Containers made of platinum are resistant to heat and reactions. Jewelers use it for settings for gems and for surfaces to be finely engraved. The finest fountain pen points are made of platinum. Some platinum compounds are used to make fluorescent screens for X-rays.

Platinum (symbol Pt) has atomic number 78. Its atomic weight is 195.09. W.J.K.

SEE ALSO: ATOM, ELEMENTS

Platyhelminthes (platt-ee-hell-MINN-theez) Platyhelminthes are animals better known as *flatworms*. With their wide, thin bodies, they look like pieces of ribbon. Some of the ocean flatworms are shaped like tree leaves. They have beautiful, striped bodies with ruffled edges.

The smallest flatworm cannot be seen except under a microscope. Some live under stones on the damp forest floor. Others cling to plants and rocks in ponds and oceans. Most of the largest, like the fluke and tapeworm, live hidden in the bodies of animals where they cause disease.

Movement from place to place is slow. Most flatworms propel themselves by beating rows of tiny *cilia,* which cover their bodies. Many secrete a carpet of *mucus,* over which they glide. Muscles help them to wriggle and squirm, and to change position. Obtaining food is difficult for a slow-moving worm. Since food is plentiful in the body of other animals, many flatworms have adopted a parasitic way of life.

The free-living flatworms are a busy, active group, found in water and on land. Most of them are *carnivores* which feed upon tiny animals. They often work slowly upon a dead animal or upon an oyster or barnacle, which cannot run away. While a few members have no DIGESTIVE SYSTEM, others have a simple digestive cavity, shaped like a glove, with three or more branching pockets. Since there is only one opening to the digestive cavity, food enters and waste is eliminated through the mouth.

The fresh-water *planaria* is perhaps the best known member of this group. The mouth is located on the bottom of the body at the end of a muscular pharynx. The animal feeds by pushing the *pharynx* or muscular, tongue-like organ outside the body cavity. Food, taken directly into the pharynx, is crushed into smaller pieces. The PLANARIA has a well-developed head with two clusters of eyes and two sensory areas on either side of the head. Planarias have great powers of regeneration. Almost any medium-sized piece will grow into a complete worm. If the head is cut down the middle, the planaria will grow two new heads.

Just as all animals must adapt to a new environment, the body of the parasitic flatworm is modified, in order that it may live inside another animal. The adult attaches itself tenaciously to the body of its host by means of suckers or sharp hooks. Since the adult no longer needs to move in search of food, it loses its outer covering of cilia, which is replaced by a thin protective cuticle. The TAPEWORM which absorbs its food directly through the body wall from its host, has neither a mouth nor a digestive system.

A few of the PARASITES spend their lives in the body of only one animal. Some *flukes* are external parasites, which live on the skin or gills of fish. Other one-host flukes are internal parasites which enter the host through openings like the mouth, anus, or excretory pore. Many are found living inside fish, amphibians, and aquatic reptiles.

Most parasitic flatworms have a complicated life history. In order to develop from egg to larva, and finally to adult form, they need to find two or more hosts in whose bodies they may pass through various stages. This is called *alternation of hosts*.

Adults of both the fluke and tapeworm usually develop in the bodies of vertebrates such as man, fish, cow, or mouse. The fluke LARVA, which passes through four larval stages, generally develops in the body of a small invertebrate animal, like the snail or copepod. The Chinese LIVER FLUKE, for example, passes through four larval stages in the body of a particular species of snail. The larva swims to the body of a fish and finally enters a human host, when raw fish is eaten by man. The tapeworm usually needs two vertebrate hosts. The larva of the beef tapeworm develops in the cow.

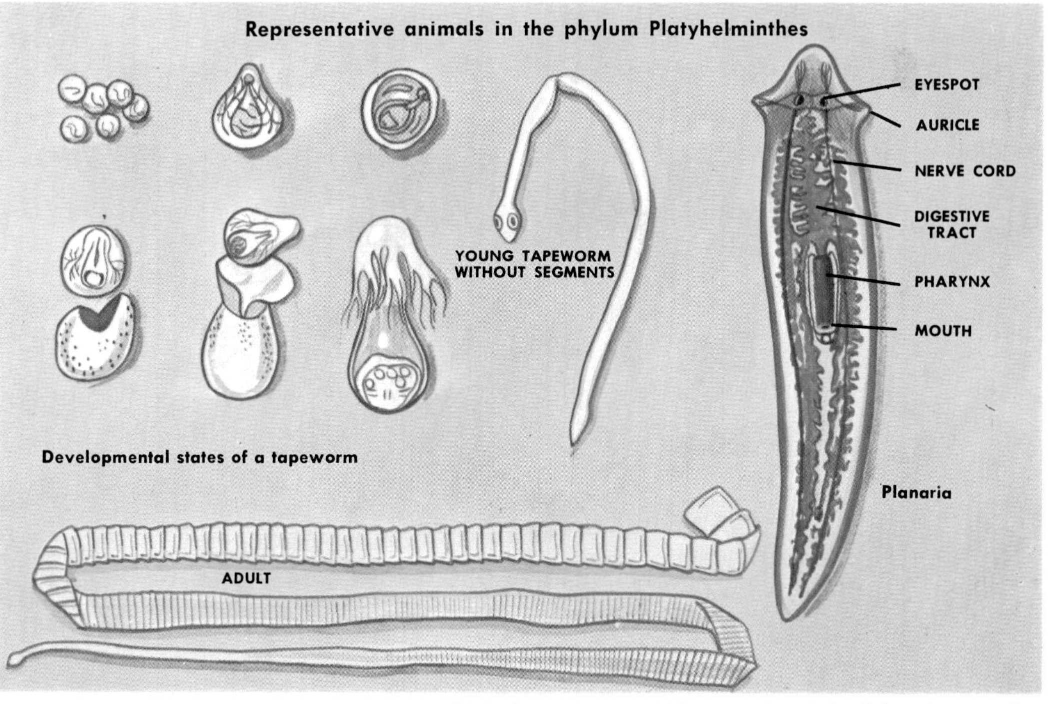

Adapted from Turtox Key card 5.5, courtesy General Biological Supply House, Chicago

When undercooked diseased beef is eaten by man, the tapeworm matures in the human intestine.

While flatworms are primitive animals, they are the first phylum in the history of life to show "two-sided" or *bilateral symmetry*. Flatworms have three body layers. The outer layer of adult parasites is often only a thick cuticle, but the free-living flatworms have a ciliated epidermis. The middle layer, or *mesoderm,* is a solid layer, containing muscles, as well as excretory and reproductive organs. While some of the free-living flatworms have well-developed nervous systems, many parasites, like the tapeworm, have sensory cells around suckers and neuromuscular cells beneath subcuticular muscles (muscles under the skin). No circulatory or breathing systems are present.

Most flatworms produce both eggs and sperm. The parasites are specialized for reproduction. Their systems are more complex than those of many higher animals. To insure reproduction of the species, these worms produce many thousands of eggs. Many of the eggs will not survive because they will be food for other animals or will not find a suitable host. E. P. L.

SEE ALSO: ANIMALS, CLASSIFICATION OF

Platypus see Duckbill

Pleiades see Taurus

Pleistocene see Cenozoic Era, Geologic time table

Pleurisy (PLOOR-uh-see) Pleurisy is an infection or inflammation between the two layers of the *pleura*. The pleura is a thin sheet of tissue that lines the chest cavity and folds back on itself enclosing each LUNG. When an infected person breathes, the two layers of the pleura scrape together, causing great pain.

Pleurisy is frequently the result of an inflammation from the *Coxsackie* virus. It causes severe chest pain when the victim inhales. This usually disappears in a few days. If the pleurisy is secondary to a lung disease (PNEUMONIA, TUBERCULOSIS, or CANCER) or occurs following rib fractures or wounds, it is serious. Pus from infection forming in the pleural space must be surgically drained. B.M.H./E.S.S.

Plexus see Nervous system

Pliocene see Cenozoic Era, Geologic time table

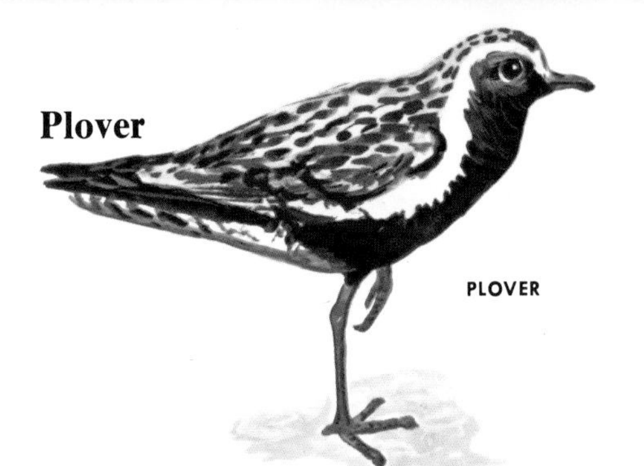

Plover Plovers are a family of long-legged shore birds. They live near water and stay near the shore. There are many different species of plovers. The family includes *killdeer, turnstones,* and *lapwings.* Plovers are often confused with SNIPE, but they have more compact bodies and shorter beaks.

The name "plover" means rain. In Europe, plovers are called rainbirds because they become noisy just before a rain. They have plump bodies, large heads, and a subdued color. They either have no toes or the toes are very small.

Plovers migrate great distances. Most of them breed in the far north and winter in the south. They often travel over 2,000 miles (3,218 kilometers) in going from one place to the other. Four fairly large, tan eggs are laid in nests made in hollows in the sand or earth. Young birds are born with down (*precocial* birds) and leave the nest soon after hatching. J.C.K.

Plum A plum tree has smooth-skinned, juicy, tart fruit. The plum is often dried to make prunes. In the United States, plums for prunes are grown in the Pacific states, where drying conditions are most favorable.

Plums are shrubs, or small trees, with white flowers, and large, smooth, clustered fruits. When dried for prunes they must be fully ripe.

Plum trees are usually bought as one-year-old trees and are planted in the fall, or early spring, in the colder climates. Plums need heavy, well-drained soil. The young trees must be pruned to shape and to develop better quality fruit.

The European plum is the most important type in the United States. The Japanese plum includes most of the varieties produced on the west coast for the fresh fruit market. Native American varieties are quite desirable in their own areas and are good in home orchards. M. R. L.

Plum tree with ripe fruit
Courtesy Society For Visual Education, Inc.

Plumeria

Plumeria (ploom-AIR-ee-uh) Flowers of this tropical tree are large and shaped like a funnel. They may be white, yellow, or pink. Leaves are simple and have a smooth margin. The sap in the stem is milky.

Plumeria is also called the *frangipani* or *temple* tree. Perfect blooms form a cluster or inflorescence. Individual FLOWERS have a five-lobed calyx and corolla. The fragrant flowers mature into a fruit composed of two follicles. Plumeria trees are relatively small, from 20 to 40 feet (6.1 to 12.2 meters) high, but they may produce leaves a foot (.3 meter) long. They belong to the dogbane or Apocynaceae family. H.J.C.

Plumule A plumule is the first bud of a new plant. A plumule is part of the embryo of a seed after fertilization. Miniature leaves surround this growing point.

The epicotyl is above where the embryo is attached to the cotyledon. It includes the tiny leaves and plumule. Hypocotyl and radicle are below the plumule. H. J. C.

Pluto Pluto is one of the nine planets in our SOLAR SYSTEM. It is the farthest from the sun and travels in a very *eccentric* (flat oval) orbit. Pluto's

Pluto has an eccentric orbit, part of which lies within the orbit of Neptune

orbit is at a slight angle to the plane of the orbits of the other planets. At one point in its orbit, Pluto is 35 million miles (56 million kilometers) within the orbit of Neptune. Pluto was not discovered until 1930. No planets beyond Pluto are known to exist. It can be seen only with a large telescope.

Pluto seems to be in a class by itself. The four inner planets are called *terrestial planets* and the next four are termed *great planets*. Pluto's mass is nearly that of the Earth's, but it appears to be much smaller, indicating a high density.

After Uranus and Neptune were discovered, astronomers thought that they had solved the mystery of the changes in Uranus' motion. They found, though, that Uranus was still not moving according to predictions. They wondered if perhaps there might be still another planet beyond Neptune. Early in the 1900's, an American astronomer Percival Lowell worked out by mathematics some approximate figures for "Planet X." Lowell's description of the planet that no one had ever seen turned out to be remarkably close to what was later discovered to be true. Although Percival Lowell looked for Planet X for several years, he never found it. He died in 1916. Other astronomers took on the search. In 1930 Clyde W. Tombaugh found the mystery planet. He used Lowell's figures and took pictures of the area of the sky that supposedly would show the planet. Pictures taken on different nights showed an object that looked like a faint star. But this "star" was in a different position on different nights. It was moving. It was the new planet.

Even through very powerful telescopes, Pluto only shows itself as a tiny point of light. It is difficult for astronomers to get reliable information about this tiny speck of light. Because of its great distance from Earth, astronomers have had a very difficult time determining its size and other characteristics. Recent observations indicate that Pluto has a diameter of about 1,367 miles (2,200 kilometers). Pluto may have a rocky core covered by ice. The planet seems to have a thin atmosphere of methane with traces of free hydrogen. Pluto has one moon, Charon, discovered in 1978. At 721 miles (1,160 kilometers) in diameter, Charon is the largest moon in the solar system in relation to its planet.

Pluto s distance from the sun ranges from 2.75 billion miles (4.42 billion kilometers) to 4.59 billion miles (7.39 billion kilometers). At these distances the sun would only appear as a very bright star in the permanently night sky. Average "dayside" temperatures would be about -370° F. (50° Kelvin or -223.3° C.). Spectroscopic studies have indicated that frozen methane (CH_4) and perhaps even neon may exist as frost on the surface of Pluto.

It takes Pluto about 248 years to make a trip around the sun. Pluto's orbit is not circular; it is elliptical. The sun is not at the focus of the ellipse. When Pluto is at its closest point to the sun, Pluto is actually inside Neptune's orbit. Then Pluto is nearer to Earth than Neptune is. From 1979 to 1999 Pluto will be nearer to Earth than Neptune will. Computer studies have revealed that over millions of years, the orbit of Pluto is not completely predictable.

All of the other planets revolve around the sun in about the same plane or level. Some of the other orbits are slightly tilted, but Pluto's orbit is inclined at a sharp angle of 17 degrees. This means that sometimes Pluto is high above the other planets in their journey around the sun and sometimes Pluto is rather far below the others.

Because it is difficult to see Pluto's disk, astronomers find it difficult to determine Pluto's period of rotation. It is thought that Pluto rotates in about 6½ days. Astronomers have not been able to discover any satellites of Pluto.

Some theories suggest that Pluto may

have had its origin not as a planet, but as a satellite of Uranus or Neptune. It may have once been a moon that went astray and later was trapped into its present orbit about the sun. Additional differences in Pluto's characteristics lead some astronomers to believe that perhaps its origin was outside of our solar system, and it wandered into the gravitational influence of the sun. Theories will continue to be debated until spacecraft can reach Pluto and provide scientists with greater detail. C.L.K./P.P.S.

SEE ALSO: NEPTUNE, SOLAR SYSTEM, URANUS

Plutonium (ploo-TOH-nee-um) Plutonium is ACTINIDE ELEMENT 94 in MENDELEEV'S PERIODIC TABLE. It is man-made, RADIOACTIVE, and fissionable. It was discovered in 1940 by GLENN T. SEABORG.

Plutonium is found in the uranium ore PITCHBLENDE in extremely small amounts. Man-made plutonium was first produced, however, by bombardment of the element URANIUM by atomic particles known as *deuterons.* Actually the element neptunium is formed first (93rd element), and a radioactive decay takes place to form plutonium. Plutonium is important in atomic energy because fission can occur when a neutron enters the plutonium nucleus.

The plutonium isotope having mass number (^{239}Pu) is a very important source of atomic energy. Uranium with a mass number of (^{238}U) is found in large amounts but can be made to fission or split only by absorbing neutrons of high energy ("fast" neutrons). The isotope (^{239}Pu) will fission when it absorbs either high energy or low energy ("slow") neutrons. On this basis, plutonium is a more efficient material than natural uranium. In a NUCLEAR REACTOR, plutonium is formed when (^{238}U) absorbs neutrons resulting from the fission of (^{235}U). An isotope of neptunium (^{239}Np) occurs as an intermediate in the reaction. The reactions are:

$$ {}^{238}_{92}\text{U} + {}^{1}_{0}\text{n} \rightarrow {}^{239}_{92}\text{U} $$

$$ {}^{239}_{92}\text{U} \rightarrow {}^{239}_{93}\text{Np} + {}^{0-1}_{1\text{e}} \quad [\textit{Beta decay}] $$

$$ {}^{239}_{93}\text{Np} \rightarrow {}^{239}_{94}\text{Pu} + {}^{0-1}_{1\text{e}} \quad [\textit{Beta decay}] $$

A reactor producing one nuclear fuel (^{239}Pu) as it uses up another nuclear fuel (^{235}U) is called a *breeder* reactor. The plutonium produced can be separated from uranium by chemical methods. But the separation of the rare (^{235}U) from the abundant (^{238}U) is more difficult because these materials are chemically identical.

As with other metals, salts of plutonium are known and have been produced in the laboratory. Among these compounds are the oxides, halides (chlorides, bromides, and iodides), and carbides. The mass number of its most stable isotope is 244. M.S.

SEE ALSO: ELEMENTS, NUCLEAR ENERGY

Lamination of plywood

Plywood Plywood is made by gluing wide thin slices, or layers, of wood together in order to make a strong wide board.

Each layer, or *ply,* is peeled from a log and so arranged that the grain will run at right angles to that of the layer above and below it. This keeps the wood from warping and splitting. The plies are glued together under pressure, either in a wet or dry state. Dry plies make a better plywood as the tendency toward shrinkage is reduced.

Varieties of plywood called *laminated* and *batten* are made by having the veneers lie perpendicular to the outside layer. Plywood is always made with an odd number of veneers, as 3 ply, 5 ply, etc.

Plywood is used where large, lightweight, strong panels are desired as in walls, doors, furniture, railroad cars, boats and boxes.

If properly glued, plywood is very weatherproof. J. M. C.

Pneumatics (new-MAT-iks) Pneumatics is the branch of physics which deals with the mechanical properties (such as density, elasticity, pressure) of air and other gases.

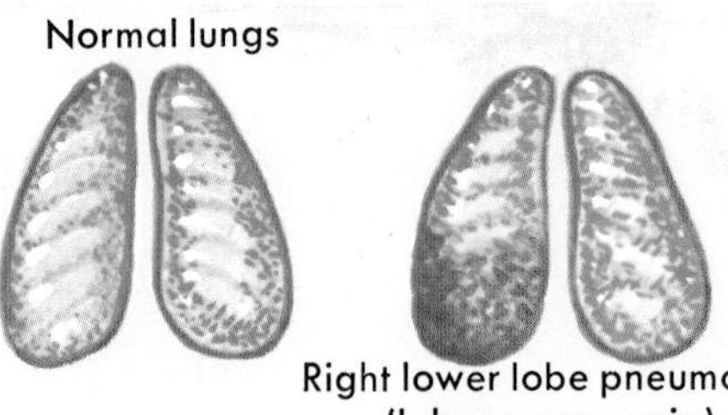

Pneumonia (nu-MOH-nyuh) Pneumonia means inflammation of the LUNG. It may be caused by infection or by chemical irritation. *Lobar* pneumonia means an entire lobe of a lung is affected. In *bronchial* pneumonia, the infection is scattered in patches throughout the lung. Because the infected lung cannot bring oxygen to the blood, a person with pneumonia is short of breath. The inflammation also causes the patient to cough.

Pneumonia almost always develops from inhalation of infected material from the nose and throat. The material may be BACTERIAL, VIRAL, or *rickettsial.* The accidental taking in of gastric juice and food particles during vomiting, for example, may cause patches of pneumonia in unconscious or debilitated persons. Oily nose drops may run into the lungs to cause *lipoid* pneumonia. Inhalation of smoke, hot gases, or CHLORINE can also cause pneumonia.

The *pneumococcus* bacteria causes the classic form of *lobar* pneumonia. The onset is usually sudden, with chills and fever following a cough that produces "rusty" (blood-tinged) sputum. Because of antibiotics, this disease is no longer the "dread disease" of the past in which the patient either "passed the crisis" or died.

Today, viral infections of the lungs are common, especially in young people. These are called "atypical pneumonias" because the symptoms and course of the disease differ from lobar pneumonia. A great number of viruses can cause pneumonitis. Examples are the *Eaton, Coxsackie,* and *adenovirus.* Atypical pneumonia is characterized by a dry, hacking, exhausting cough, and sometimes high fever. Antibiotics are useful in treating certain viral pneumonias.

Psittacosis pneumonia is contracted from infected parrots and parakeets. *Streptococcal* pneumonia often complicates influenza. More serious is *staphyococcal* pneumonia; it can be resistant to many antibiotics. Pneumonia is especially serious in the very young or very old. Underlying diabetes, alcoholism, and heart disease may be fatal for a person with pneumonia. A new anti-pneumococcal vaccine has recently been developed to protect the sick and the weak from developing a fatal pneumonia. B.M.H.

SEE ALSO: LUNGS, RESPIRATORY SYSTEM

Poi see Taro

Poinciana (poyn-see-AN-uh) Poinciana trees are small, broad-topped trees with large, brightly colored flowers. They grow in the tropical areas of the world. They belong to the pea family.

The *royal poinciana* is one of the most striking tropical trees. It grows 20 to 40 feet (6.1 to 12.2 meters) tall, spreading wide at its top. Its leaves are 1 to 2 feet (.3 to .6 meter) long, each divided into many small leaflets. The five petals of the flower are orange or scarlet and have uneven edges. Ten stamens stand up from the petals. The seeds are contained in pods which are flat and from 6 inches to 2 feet (15.2 to 61 centimeters) long. This species is native to Madagascar but is cultivated in southern Florida and other warm areas where the colorful plant blooms mostly in the summer.

The *dwarf poinciana* is a 10-foot (3-meter) shrub with prickly branches. It has delicate leaves and orange or yellow flowers, each 2 inches (5.1 centimeters) across. It is widely distributed throughout the tropics. E.R.B.

Poinciana tree and scarlet flowers

F. A. Blashfield

White poinsettias

Poinsettia (poyn-SETT-ee-uh) The poinsettia plant has small, yellow flowers. They are surrounded by white, red, or purple *bracts,* which look like leaves or petals. They are not part of the flower itself.

Leaves are simple, alternate, oval, and tapering. The stem contains a milky juice. Poinsettias grow between 2 to 6 feet (.6 to 1.8 meters) tall. In frost-free areas it may become a shrub over 10 feet (3 meters).

Flowers form a cluster. Bracts surround the cluster and can reach a diameter of 6 to 8 inches (15.2 to 20.3 centimeters). The pistil develops into a FRUIT called a *schizocarp.*

Originally, the poinsettia came from Mexico and Central America. Dr. Poinsett, for whom the plant is named, was responsible for bringing it to the United States. Poinsettias belong to the spurge or Euphorbiaceae family. H.J.C.

Poison Any substance which, when taken into the body, affects health or causes death is a poison. Poisons are very common. Every household contains poisonous items such as ammonia, medicines, and kerosene. Chemical warfare utilizes poisonous gases.

Poisons are classified according to the bodily part affected. Most poisons, if used in proper quantities or for the original purpose, are of great help to mankind.

A large group of poisons are called *nerve poisons* because of the effect on the nervous system of the body. Among nerve poisons are *strychnine, chloroform, alcohol,* and *belladonna.* These poisons cause delirium, convulsions, and stupors.

Irritant poisons are caustic poisons caused by *acids, alkalies,* and mercuric and phosphorus compounds. The irritant poison taken into the body burns the throat, the passage to the stomach, and the intestine.

Poison gases are used in wartime or are sometimes released in an industrial accident. These gases can stop the action of the heart or eliminate the oxygen supply to the body.

Numerous poisons are found around the house. Many household cleaners such as ammonia, lye, turpentine, and kerosene, if taken by mouth, are poisonous. Extremely dangerous are the very common INSECTICIDES. If food is neither prepared nor refrigerated properly, food poisoning may occur. Medicines are often taken in too large dosages or by mistake. Most medicines, if not taken as directed, will cause serious illness or death. The type of deadly mushroom called the *death cup* may be eaten by unsuspecting people. Most poisons have a known *antidote* which, if given promptly, will offset the effects of the poison.

The American Red Cross, the National Safety Council, Scout organizations, as well as many other medical and civic organizations, sustain a continuous campaign to prevent accidental poisoning.

Fundamentally important to remember is the prevention of accidental poisoning. Several safety rules are: (1) keep all household cleaners, insecticides, and medicines out of the reach of small children; (2) poisonous medicine and drugs, labeled with a skull and crossbones, should be locked up; (3) older children should be trained as to the dangers of poisons; (4) all unnecessary poisonous items should be thrown away; (5) the family should know the first-aid treatment for poisons. P. F. D.

SEE ALSO: ANTIDOTE, ARSENIC, CHEMICAL WARFARE, FIRST AID

For emergency only

UNIVERSAL ANTIDOTE

Two parts—Burned toast, powdered
One part —Milk of magnesia
One part —Strong brewed tea

The burned toast supplies absorbent carbon; the milk of magnesia is mildly alkaline buffer against acids; the tea has tannic acid that neutralizes alkalies.

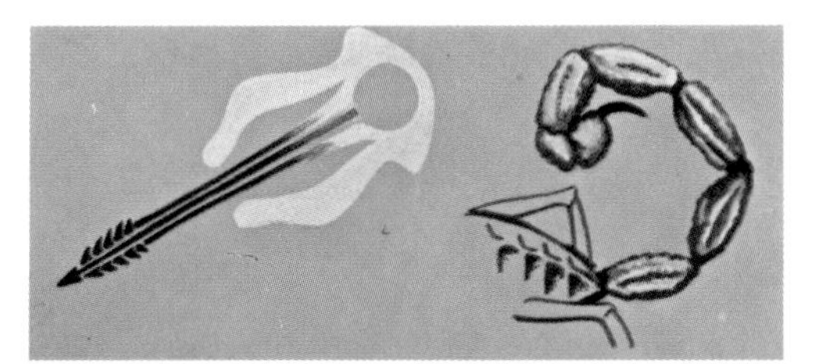

Poison glands of a bee (left) and a scorpion (right)

Poison gland A poison gland is a specialized gland found in some animals. This gland produces *venom*. Poison glands are used for protection or as a means of getting food. Venom may cause pain, dizziness, swelling, paralysis, or even death of the victim.

Among animals that have poison glands are some SNAKES. Their fangs contain saliva that can poison other animals when it is injected into the blood stream. Scorpions kill their prey with a poison stinger at the end of their tail. Toads have small poison glands in their skins. The GILA MONSTER bites, and venom flows from glands in its lower jaw into the wound. BEES, wasps, and hornets are well-known for their effective stingers. The sting ray lies on the ocean or river bottom and with its tail drives a sharp spine and poison into its enemy. The Portuguese man-of-war floats like a balloon and has tentacles with stinging cells, reaching down underneath. Some tropical catfish have poison glands in their spines. M. R. L.

Poison ivy Everyone should know what poison ivy looks like in order to avoid it. The tissues of this plant contain a poisonous oil which causes fever and itching, burning and blistering of the skin.

Poison ivy belongs to the cashew family. Although it may be a low shrub, it is often a vine climbing upon tree trunks or other supports. It does not twine like many vines. Some vines cling to supports with *tendrils.* These are modified stems, leaves or parts of leaves. Poison ivy clings with roots growing out from the stem. Its leaf is compound, made up of three shiny green leaflets that change to bright red in autumn. The small flowers are followed by fruits that are *drupes* but look like whitish berries. J. C. K.

SEE ALSO: POISON OAK

Poison oak The leaves of the poison oak plant look much like those of the poison ivy except they are wavy on the edges. They come in groups of three leaflets, are light green above but lighter underneath, and are thickly covered with fine hairs.

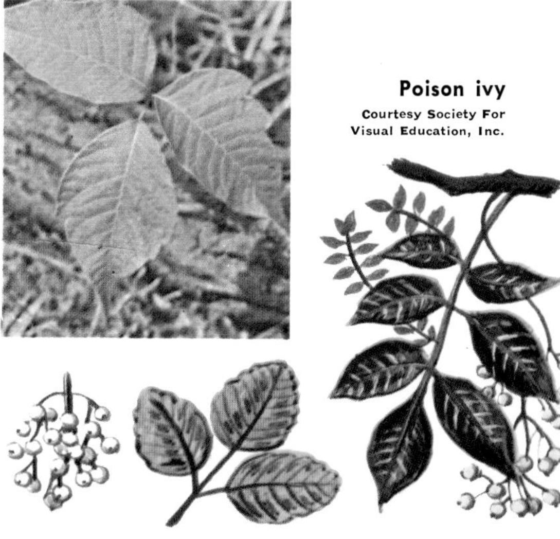

Poison ivy
Courtesy Society For Visual Education, Inc.
Poison oak
Poison sumac

One form of poison oak that grows on the Pacific Coast of North America is a shrub about 8 feet (2.4 meters) tall. Another variety is found in the southern states.

Contact with poison oak will cause the same itching and blistering of the skin as poison ivy, and requires the same treatment. The skin should be scrubbed with hot water and alkaline soap immediately. J. K. K.

Poison sumac see Sumac

Pokeweed see Wild flowers

Polar bear see Bear

Polar climate see Climate

Polar easterlies The heating and cooling of the earth's surface, plus the rotating movement of the earth upon its axis, causes massive movements of air. Scientists have observed air movements and classified them into what is called the *planetary wind system.* The

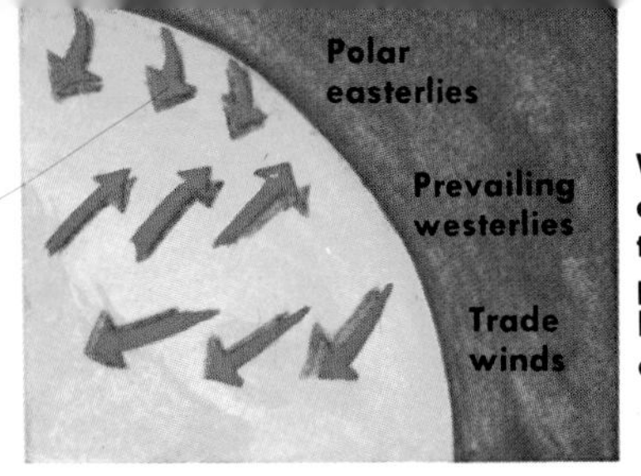

When polar easterlies move south, they interact with prevailing westerlies and cause cyclonic storms.

polar easterlies are part of that system of winds that are characteristic of the polar regions.

Weather in the middle latitudes, where most people live, is greatly affected by the polar winds. When the pressure is sufficient, great air waves break out of the polar zones and move into the middle latitudes. As they travel toward the equator, they are deflected to the west in the Northern Hemisphere. They interact with the *prevailing westerlies* on their way east, causing *cyclonic* storms. When polar air is caught in the westerlies and carried eastward, it becomes traveling *anticyclones,* or highs. E.M.N.

SEE ALSO: WEATHER, WESTERLIES

Polar regions see Antarctica; Arctic; Earth; Poles, North and South

Polar wandering Polar wandering is the movement of the earth's *magnetic* pole position. Generally, magnetic north does not correspond to *true* or geographic north. Its location has varied with time.

The earth's magnetic field is believed to be the result of electric currents that are generated in the core. The earth's rotation produces a di-pole magnetic field that is centered around the rotational axis. The present dipole field is located 11.5 degrees from the true north of the rotational axis. The earth's magnetic field periodically reverses its polarity, and weakens in intensity. Recent intensity drops in the present magnetic field suggest a coming reversal. P.P.S.

SEE ALSO: EARTH, ELECTRICITY, MAGNETISM

Polaris (poh-LAIR-iss) Polaris is the star that is always almost directly above the North Pole. It is also called the *Pole Star*. For many years sailors and explorers in the Northern Hemisphere have used this star to find directions. When a person faces Polaris,

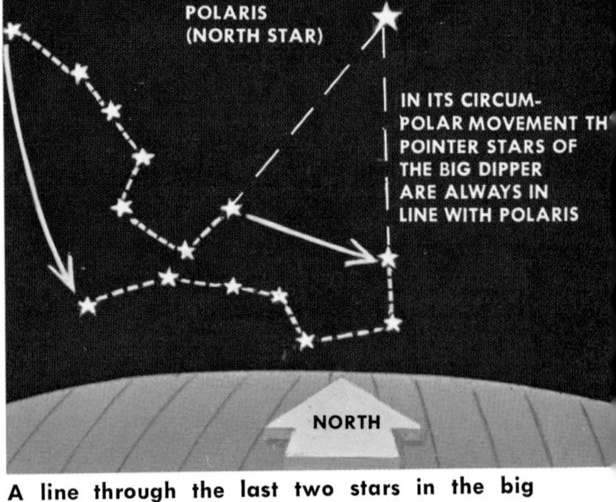

A line through the last two stars in the big dipper will point directly at Polaris

he is facing true north. Polaris is sometimes called the North Star.

Polaris is not one of the brightest stars in the sky. It can be found easily, however, with the help of the "pointer stars." The pointers are two stars in the Big Dipper that point to Polaris. They are the two stars that form the side of the dipper which is farthest from the handle. A line through these two stars leads to Polaris. Polaris is the last star in the handle of the Little Dipper. The dippers are parts of the constellation *Ursa Major* and *Ursa Minor*.

Polaris cannot be seen at all in the Southern Hemisphere. In the Northern Hemisphere it is visible the year round. Polaris is not exactly above the North Pole. If it were, it would not seem to move at all. As the earth rotates, however, Polaris traces a very small circle around the celestial North Pole. The constellations near Polaris are called *circumpolar* constellations. They seem to move in a circle around Polaris.

Besides helping to find directions, Polaris can tell a person in the Northern Hemisphere what latitude he is in. The degree of the angle from the horizon to Polaris is about the same degree of latitude that the observer is from the equator. At the equator this angle is zero for Polaris is on the horizon. At the North Pole, the angle is 90 degrees. Polaris is directly overhead.

Polaris has not always been the pole star. Many years ago, *Thuban* was the star used to find the north direction. The earth's axis changes its direction very slowly. It is moving away from Polaris now. In about 12,000 years *Vega,* a very bright star, will be the north star. C. L. K.

SEE ALSO: BIG AND LITTLE DIPPERS, CONSTELLATION, URSA MAJOR AND MINOR

Polaris see Missile, Submarine

Polarization (poh-ler-uh-ZAY-shun) When the *electrodes* in a *voltaic cell* or any other cell become surrounded by atoms of nonconducting gases, the internal resistance of the cell increases. The result of the increased internal resistance is a drop in the emf (electromotive force) of the cell. This decreased emf is due to *polarization* of the electrodes.

The process of polarization in a voltaic cell is somewhat as follows: The electrodes of the cell, in which the CATHODE is copper and the ANODE is zinc, are placed in a weak solution of sulfuric acid. Inside the cell some positive hydrogen ions flow toward the copper, where they combine with free electrons to form neutral atoms of hydrogen. These neutral hydrogen atoms cling to the copper as a gas and coat it entirely, thus causing the copper electrode to act like an electrode of hydrogen. However, the potential difference between zinc and hydrogen is less than it is between zinc and copper and the emf of the cell is reduced. Due to the decreased emf the cell cannot supply as much current to an external circuit as before; hence, it is polarized. A. E. L.

Polaroid see Land, Edwin

Pole (general) A pole is either end of an *axis*. For instance, in physics either end of a MAGNET is its pole. In electricity the pole is one of the two *terminals* of the current source. In biology, the pole is one of the opposite ends of the organism or cell which are physiologically different.

Pole, magnetic see Magnet, Electricity

Poles, North and South The earth turns, or rotates, on an axis which is pictured as an imaginary slanted line running through its center. The end point of the imaginary line in the Northern Hemisphere, or northern half of the world, is the North Pole. The end point of the line in the Southern Hemisphere is the South Pole.

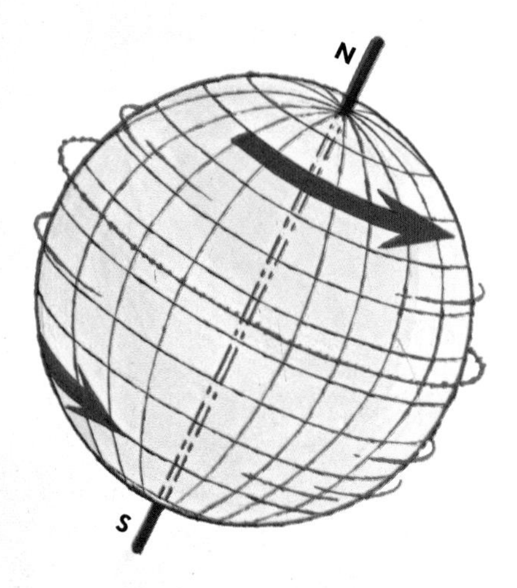

The poles are at the end of the imaginary axis around which the earth rotates

Many times when people speak of the North Pole or the South Pole, they mean the general regions around the end points of the earth's axis. These are often referred to as the *true* or geographical poles. The earth also has a magnetic pole which is based on the direction of *polarity* of its magnetic field. The two do not correspond in location, but vary by 11.5 degrees.

For years the poles have been the goal of many explorers. On April 6, 1909, the U.S. explorer ROBERT E. PEARY, his assistant Matthew Henson, and four Eskimos reached the North Pole. These men were the first to see the sun and stars go around the sky in horizontal circles. Peary had 32 observations to substantiate his claim.

On December 16, 1911, the Norwegian ROALD AMUNDSEN and four companions crossed the South Pole. On May 9, 1926, RICHARD BYRD (U.S.) led an air expedition which successfully crossed the North Pole. Especially since the INTERNATIONAL GEOPHYSICAL YEAR (1957-58) many more expeditions have penetrated the polar regions by land and undersea. The first undersea exploration was made by the atomic-powered submarine *Nautilus*. E.M.N.

Polecat see Weasel

Poliomyelitis (pole-ih-oh-MI-eh-LIE-tis) This disease is also known as *infantile paralysis*. It is an *infectious* disease that is also *contagious*. Inhaling the virus into the nose and throat produces disease. Much more often, however, the virus enters the mouth by transfer from contaminated fingers or infected water or food. Very rarely, the disease is spread by flies and insects. The virus multiplies in the intestinal tract and fecal contamination becomes the source of spread. The disease can cause paralysis of the body muscles.

The incidence of polio infection rose steadily between 1918 and 1941. It went sharply and alarmingly upward after 1941.

There are three types of polio virus. Being immune to one type does not make a person immune to the others. Most polio infections are nonparalytic. In this type of polio, a person has a low-grade fever, complains of headache and stiffness in the muscles, loses his appetite, and may vomit. After this passes, recovery is complete. An immunity to this virus has been developed.

One case in 1,000 is paralytic. The virus breaks into the blood stream from the intestines, where it has been multiplying, and is carried to the brain and/or the spinal cord. It settles in the nerve cells responsible for muscle movement. Once the nerve cells die, the corresponding muscles can no longer be moved. If the lower part of the brain is affected (bulbar type), swallowing and breathing may be impossible, and mechanical ventilation becomes necessary. In the encephalitic type, a coma develops.

The *Salk vaccine* for poliomyelitis was introduced in 1954. Dr. Albert Sabin has since developed a vaccine that is taken by mouth. This vaccine is now in general use, and if all children would be immunized at the proper times, the disease would virtually disappear.

B.M.H./E.S.S.

SEE ALSO: IRON LUNG; MEDULLA OBLONGATA; NERVOUS SYSTEM; SALK, JONAS; VACCINE

Pollen (PAHL-enn) If a lily or a dandelion flower is dusted across one's hand, a yellow powder can be seen. That powder is made of tiny grains of pollen.

Pollen forms in the *anthers* at the ends of the male part of the flower called the *stamen*. If the flower develops properly, some of the pollen grains are dusted onto the head of the female part of the flower called the PISTIL. From each pollen grain a slender hair-like tube grows down through the pistil. A pollen nucleus travels through the tube and unites with the little seed-to-be, the *ovule*, in the ovary (the seed case).

V. V. N.

SEE ALSO: ALLERGY; PLANT; REPRODUCTION, SEXUAL

✳ THINGS TO DO

HOW DOES THE POLLEN GET TO THE EGG TO FERTILIZE IT?

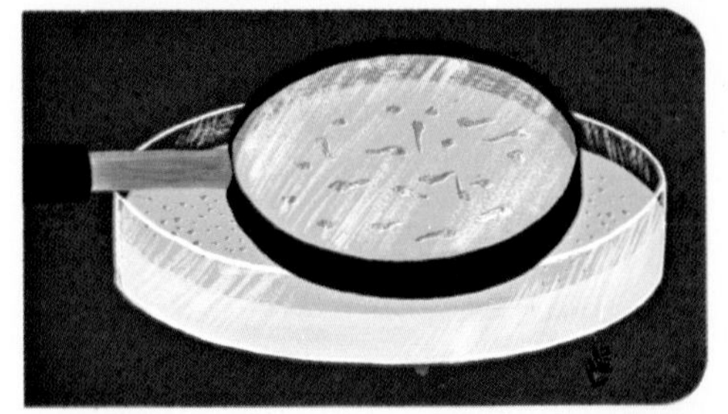

1. **Make a thin sugar solution. This will serve as a medium in which the pollen grains can grow.**
2. **Locate a freshly-opened flower. Place the solution in a shallow dish and shake the stamens (the stalk usually with yellow knobs) over the solution. Cover the dish and permit it to stand for an hour.**
3. **Using a hand lens observe the long extension which has sprouted from each grain. This is the pollen tube which grows down the pistil until its nucleus joins the nucleus of the egg.**

Pollination (PAHL-ih-nay-shun) Seeds develop after flowering only if pollen is transferred from the male part of the flower (*stamen*) to the female part of the flower (*pistil*) of the same kind of plant. This transfer of pollen to the ovule (*future seed*) in gymnosperms, or to the receptive structure of the ovary (*the stigma*) in flowering

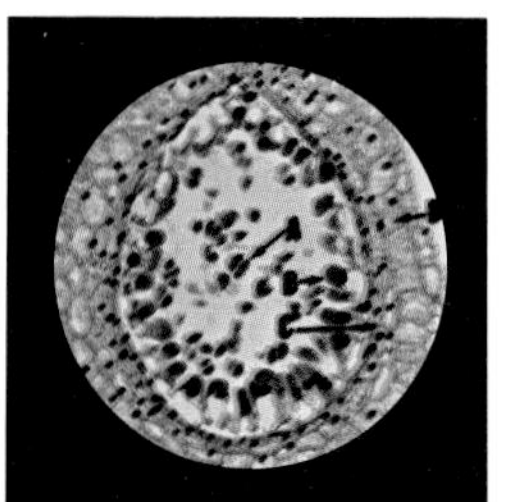

Pollen forms in sacs in the anther. A—pollen tetrad; B—pollen mother cells; C and D outer layers of cells which dry and crack open to release pollen

Photo-micrographs by National Teaching Aids, Inc.

plants, is called *pollination.* Without pollination, there would be no new seed for a new plant.

There are two basic types of pollination. They are called *self-pollination* and *cross-pollination.* Self-pollination is the transfer of pollen from the STAMEN to the PISTIL in the same flower or to the pistil of another flower on the same plant. If pollen from the stamen of one plant is transferred to the pistil of another plant, it is cross-pollination.

When pollen is transferred from one plant to another in cross-pollination, an outside agent or help is needed. The chief agents of pollination are insects, other animals, wind, and water.

BEES are the chief insect pollinators. Moths, butterflies, and certain kinds of flies also visit flowers regularly and in so doing bring about cross-pollination.

Insects visit the flowers to obtain sweet *nectar,* which is secreted deep in the flower from special glands at the base of the petals. The plump, hairy body of the bee is ideal for this process. When the bee tries to reach the nectar glands, located at the base of the flower, it must rub its hairy body against the male anthers of the stamen. These are in most cases located near the entrance of the flower. Then as the insect visits the next flower, some of the pollen is rubbed against the sticky stigma of the female pistil. At the same time a new supply of pollen is brushed off from the stamen onto the bee.

Flowers have brightly-colored petals and sweet odors which attract insects. Nectar guides in some flowers may be brightly colored strips located on the petals. Also flowers arranged in showy clusters make them more noticeable to traveling insects passing by.

There is one type of bird that assists in pollination. The little HUMMINGBIRD feeds on the nectar of certain types of flowers. It has a long bill and a long tongue to reach down into the nectar glands while it hovers with its delicate wings overhead.

Flowers of wind-pollinated plants are much less striking in beauty than those pollinated by insects. They are usually in dense clusters at the ends of branches. Petals are lacking, and the flowers seldom have any nectar. The stamens are long and produce a large amount of pollen light in weight. The pistils are also long and the stigma large and often sticky, so that they are able to catch wind-blown pollen grains. Pines, cottonwoods, willows, walnuts, corn, oats, and other wind-pollinated plants fill the air with pollen when their stamens are ripe. Some people are allergic to the pollen. V. V. N.

SEE ALSO: FLOWERS

Pollution Pollution is a change in the environment that makes it impure or unclean. Usually the changes occur through human activities. Most of the changes are poisonous or harmful to life processes.

Pollution occurs when waste products are added to the environment. Pollutants can be solids, liquids, or gases. Pollutants are everywhere—in the air, in water ways, and in the soil.

Pollutants that occur in the air can be in the form of solid residue from burning fuels or from industrial processes. These solids are called PARTICULATE MATTER. Fine droplets of liquid pollutants, called *aerosols,* are also present in the air. These droplets can come from natural sources, such as the sea, or from man-made sources, such as spray cans. The particulate matter and aerosols range from microscopic to very large sizes.

The burning of fuels produces very high temperatures. At these temperatures the nitrogen in the air is converted to nitrogen oxides. The nitrogen oxides combine with rain to form acid rains. Nitrogen oxides also play a role in the production of *ozone.* Some other gaseous pollutants produced by burning fuels are carbon monoxide, carbon dioxide, and sulfur oxides.

The control of two air pollutants is now in effect. The use of lead in gasoline has decreased. The use of *freon,* which may destroy upper level ozone, is also declining.

Advances in technology and an increase in population have accelerated the need for fresh water. The awareness in the decline of available fresh water has resulted in a strong effort to improve water waste treatment.

Improving conditions in the purity of our water ways is a good reflection of our improved treatment of waste water. Highly polluted bodies of water, such as Lake Erie, are showing remarkable improvements. However, much remains to be done.

Some effort is being made to recycle waste materials and also to burn them with fuel to produce electrical energy. A.J.H.

SEE ALSO: AIR POLLUTION, CONSERVATION OF NATURE, GARBAGE

Polonium (puh-LOH-nee-um) Polonium is a chemical element. It is radioactive, like uranium and radium. Its symbol is Po and its atomic number is 84. The mass number of its most stable isotope is 209.

Polonium was discovered by Pierre and Marie Curie in 1898 in some samples of uranium they had obtained from pitchblende. Madame Curie named it after her native land, Poland.

Polonium is mainly used to produce neutron sources. It is also used in spark plugs and in devices to eliminate static.

Polonium is found in all uranium minerals, and can be obtained by separating it from uranium residues. It can be produced by bombarding bismuth with neutrons. C.L.K.

SEE ALSO: ELEMENTS

Polycotyledon (pohl-ih-cot-uh-LEE-dun) *Cotyledons* are seed leaves. The food supply of the seed is usually in the form of one, two, or many cotyledons. The term "polycotyledon" refers to seeds that have more than two seed leaves. Pines, spruces, hemlocks, and other cone-bearing trees are polycotyledons.

SEE: COTYLEDON, GYMNOSPERMS

Polygon see Geometry

Polymer Molecules of the same kind can be chemically joined together to form a single larger molecule. The new, heavier molecule is made up of the same elements in the same proportions. Its molecular weight is a multiple of the original molecule. This new molecule is called a "polymer."

SEE: CHEMISTRY, PLASTICS

Polymorphism Polymorphism is the occurrence of a plant or animal in different forms or colors. A chemical substance like sulfur is polymorphous when it exists in several crystalline forms.

Polyps Polyps are *coelenterates* of the class *Anthozoa.* They are also the attached forms of some coelenterates which have two forms. They are cylindrical, attached at one end, and have a mouth at the other end.

SEE: COELENTERATA

Pomegranate The pomegranate tree has been known to man for thousands of years. It is a tree or tall shrub that grows only in tropical or semitropical lands. In the United States it grows best in southern areas.

Small clusters of reddish-orange flowers bloom in the spring and are followed by a reddish or deep yellow fruit called pomegranate. This fruit is the size of a large orange. The outside covering, or rind, of the pomegranate is hard, but inside this sectioned fruit are many seeds surrounded by juicy pulp. J. A. D.

Pome A pome is a type of fruit. Apple, pear, and quince are fruits classified as pomes. The fleshy part that surrounds the core is the part of the pome that is eaten.

Cross section of a typical pome, the apple

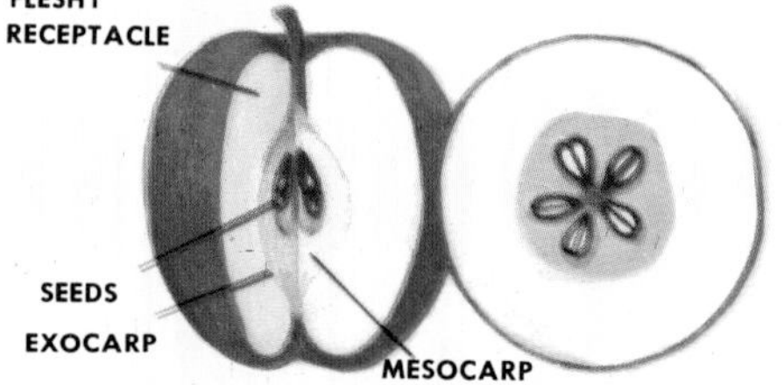

Chicago Natural History Museum

Pompano

Pompano Pompano is the name given to a group of fish found mainly along the Atlantic coastline and in the West Indies. They include the common pompano, sometimes called the *butterfish,* the round pompano and a larger variety, the jack pompano. The butterfish is popular as a food fish.

Pond A pond is a body of still water that is usually smaller than a lake. Many plants and animals live in, on, and around this natural community.

Rooted plants grow in the water along the shallow edge. Aquatic insects, amphibian larvae, small crustaceans, and fish are plentiful. Fowl and mammals use a pond as a drinking hole.

The bottom of a pond may be muddy, sandy, or rocky. The pH varies with the soil and affects the type of life that can live in this ecosystem.

Cooling ponds are created for nuclear power plants. This type of pond can be put to use if stocked with algae, fish and other life that thrive in warm waters.

A temporary pond fills during the spring rains but dries up in late summer and fall. Only living things with short life cycles can exist in this habitat. H.J.C.

Pons see Brain, Nervous system

Pontoon bridge see Bridges

Popcorn The grain of popcorn is long, oval, and thinner than that of other types of CORN. Its hull or fruit wall is hard, tough, and almost moisture-tight. Moist starch fills the inside.

Poplar Poplars are fast-growing but short-lived trees. They form great forests in lowlands and on the slopes of mountains. They have broad, heart-shaped, leathery leaves that are pale-green on the surface and silvery on the underside. Flowers and fruits form in thick hanging or upright clusters. The wood of the poplar is soft, lightweight, and brittle. It is most valuable for paper pulp.

Poplars are DECIDUOUS trees with alternate, simple LEAVES that are serrated. The fact that the leaves have palmate venation and long petioles (stems) makes them restless in the wind. Each FLOWER in the dioecious (separate sexes) catkins lacks petals. The calyx is either reduced or missing. Flowers are wind pollinated. The dry dehiscent FRUIT is a thin-walled, valved capsule that bursts open at maturity. Often the seeds have cottony hairs or down.

Lombardy poplar is a thin, tall tree about 50 feet (15 meters) tall. Its branches run almost parallel with the trunk. *Quaking aspen* is a poplar 40 feet (12 meters) high or less. It has white or yellow-green, smooth bark. *White* or *silver* poplar averages 70 feet (21 meters) tall. Its whitish leaves have shallow, lobed margins. The *cottonwood,* another poplar, often reaches heights of over 100 feet (30 meters). Poplars are in the willow or Salicaceae family. H.J.C.

Poppy This is the common name for a group of herbs with large, showy flowers that may be white, orange, purple, or various shades of red. Stems are often hairy and contain a milky juice.

Among the many varieties of poppies, there is the *opium poppy,* an annual herb 2 to 4 feet (.6 to 1.2 meters) tall. It is native to Western Asia and is cultivated extensively in China and India. The dull green leaves may be 10 inches (25.4 centimeters) long. The large single flower may be purple or red. It has two sepals, four petals, many stamens, and a compound pistil. The pistil matures into a capsule fruit that releases seeds in the same way that salt comes from a shaker. The minute seeds are bluish-black.

The milky juice that comes from the unripe fruit is called *latex.* When the latex is dried and processed, it yields OPIUM, a narcotic. *Morphine* and *codeine,* pain-relieving drugs, are also refined from it.

Poppies are grown as annuals and perennials. The family Papaveraceae is commonly known as the poppy family. H. J. C.

SEE ALSO: OPIUM; PLANTS, MEDICINAL

Poppy seed Poppy seeds are the tiny seeds that come from the fruit capsule. They are used to flavor certain foods. The walnut-flavored seeds used today are non-narcotic.

Pressing poppy seeds without heat produces an edible, white, bland oil. Pressing poppy seeds under heat yields a red oil used in paints and soaps. H. J. C.

Porcelain (PORS-uh-luhn) Porcelain is the finest and most expensive type of pottery. It is usually white and *translucent,* meaning that light will shine through it.

Porcelain is made of a mixture of *kaolin* and *feldspar.* These materials are finely ground and washed and then mixed into a clay. The clay is then worked and kneaded. When the clay reaches the proper consistency, it is shaped into the desired piece either on a potter's wheel or in a mold. If the piece is to have a handle and spout, these are separately molded and attached to the piece with the clay. Then it is set aside to dry, after which it is baked in a kiln or oven at a comparatively low temperature. The baked piece is known as a *biscuit.* The biscuit is then dipped in *glaze* and again fired at a very high temperature.

The secret of making porcelain was discovered in China. The earliest pieces date to about 900 A.D. Porcelain was introduced to Europe in the 15th century. Various Europeans tried unsuccessfully to duplicate this highly-prized chinaware. It wasn't until 1709 that Boettger, a chemist to the Elector of Saxony, succeeded in discovering the materials that compose porcelain. W. J. K.

Porcupine (PAWR-kyuh-pyne) Often called *quill pigs,* porcupines are rodents, animals that gnaw. Unlike other rodents, porcupines have coarse hair mixed with long, stiff quills. The sharp tips of the quills are pointed backward like the end of a fishhook. These slow-moving animals have short legs, broad

Courtesy Society For Visual Education, Inc.

North American porcupine (above) and prehensile-tailed South American (below)

tails, and thick-set bodies. Although found in many kinds of forests, they prefer evergreen forests.

The barbed quills, which are controlled by muscles in the skin, are loosely attached to the porcupine and easily catch on anything which touches them. Porcupines cannot throw their quills as is commonly believed. The porcupine often slaps at its enemy with its powerful tail, causing many of the long quills to become imbedded in the enemy's skin. Once imbedded, they are very difficult and painful to remove because of their barbs. Some enemies of the porcupine, such as the fox, lynx, coyote, and mountain lion, attempt to turn the porcupine over on its back; however, this is difficult to do because the porcupine is able to roll itself up into a compact spiny ball.

Porcupines are gnawing mammals (rodents), feeding mainly on the leaves, buds, and bark of trees and the roots and stems of tender plants. They are especially fond of salt. They are excellent climbers and frequently climb trees searching for food.

Porcupines have one to three babies each year in early summer. They are usually born under a rock ledge, in a crevice or cave. The babies are large and well-developed at birth, having fur, spines, and teeth. They can live alone in just one week.

There are several species of porcupines. The Canadian and the yellow-haired or European porcupine are two. The Canadian porcupine, found throughout North America, is about 3 feet (.9 meter) long, weighing up to 40 pounds (18 kilograms). The European species is smaller. D.J.A.

SEE ALSO: RODENTIA

Pore see Skin, Sweat gland

Buchsbaum

Tan sponge

Porifera (poh-RIFF-er-uh) Most people use a cloth for scrubbing cars or for washing windows. But some people use an animal, better known as a *sponge*. Although there are many different kinds of sponges, all sponges are covered with thousands of tiny holes or pores. The name *porifera* means "pore-bearer."

People who have used the bath sponge know that it is light in weight. It also remains tough, even when it is wet. The bath sponge has a soft, elastic skeleton of *spongin*. All sponges are held up by stiff, outside skeletons. However, most sponges have a scratchy skeleton of sharp chalk or glass needles.

All sponges live in water. Most of them live in the ocean. Many of those in the warm, shallow oceans have beautiful colors —pinks, scarlets, and greens. Sponges which live either in fresh water or many thousand feet under the ocean are usually colored brown or gray.

The members of this phylum used to be called "plants" or "plant-animals." Adult sponges do not move from place to place. Like plants, they attach themselves to solid surfaces, such as rocks, ground, wharfs, and even the backs of crabs. While many are shaped like branching plants, others look like vases, tubes or cups. Since most sponges live in colonies, they spread out over large areas like thick, flat cushions of moss.

A sponge is like a small, filtering plant. Water enters continually through small pores on the sides of the body. Inside the sponge, it passes into a large, hollow cavity or through an elaborate system of canals. As oxygen and small organisms are removed, wastes and carbon dioxide are passed into the water. From one or more large holes at the top of the body, water leaves in a steady jet stream.

A sponge may also be thought of as a small community of cells, working together in groups. Each group is specialized for carrying out a particular duty. The flat outer cells, which fit closely together like floor tiles, are the protective cells. *Collar* cells line the internal cavity. At the free end, this unusual cell has a long whip-like *flagellum,* protruding from a delicate collar of *protoplasm*. As the flagella beat, they drive water through the inner channels and pull food particles into the collar.

Between the inner and outer cells, there is a jelly-like, non-living substance. Embedded in this are the *mesenchyme* cells, which move like the AMEBA. Some of them receive the partly-digested food from the collar cells, digest it further, and transport it throughout the body. They probably also pass waste materials to the surface. Specialized mesenchyme cells, shaped like hollow rings, are called *pore cells*. These form the openings of pores which lead to the internal cavity.

Perhaps the most important duty of the mesenchyme cells is to secrete the skeleton which supports this great mass of cells. Sponges are classified according to the shape and composition of the needles and fibers of the skeleton. *Chalk,* or *calcareous,* sponges have needles, or *spicules,* of *calcium carbonate*. Since the needles are com-

✳ THINGS TO DO

OBSERVING LIVE SPONGES

Take a hike to a nearby pond or stream to look for live sponges. It is a little difficult to find the grayish mass, usually no larger than a moth ball clinging to sticks or stones in the water. Pick up the object they are attached to and place it in a jar of the pond water. Transfer them to an aquarium or larger container filled with the water in which they were originally living. Observe for a few days and then return the sponges to their natural habitat. They will not live long in captivity.

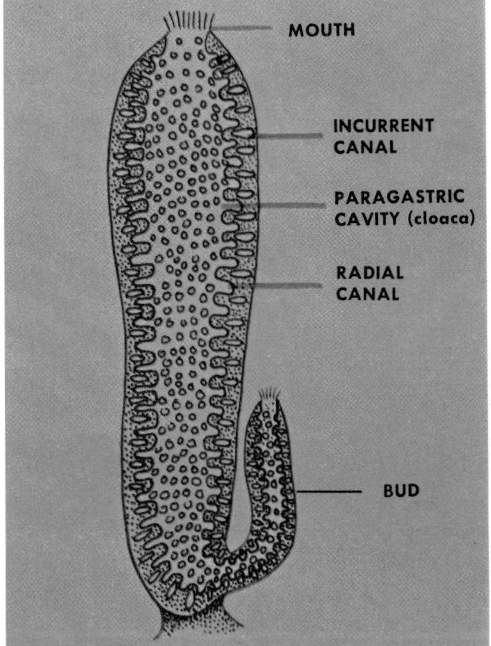

Longitudinal section of a sponge

monly shaped like a "T" or a "Y", they interlock and overlap. Most chalk sponges are small marine animals with drab color. Found in the deepest ocean water, the true *glass* sponges have beautiful six-rayed spicules of silica.

Four-fifths of all sponges belong to the class of *horn* sponges. Included are all glass sponges without six-rayed spicules, as well as sponges with horny, elastic skeletons, made of a protein secretion, called *spongin*. A few members have skeletons of both silica and spongin. Apart from the bath sponge, the horny sponges have little commercial value since the skeleton collects foreign matter, such as bits of rock.

Any portion of the sponge is able to produce an entire new animal. Some sponges reproduce asexually by budding and branching. However, all sponges are able to reproduce sexually. Eggs and sperms may be produced within the same individual, or within separate individuals. Since the free-swimming larva moves about before it settles down to become an adult, sponges are distributed over a wide area. E. P. L.

SEE ALSO: AMEBA; ANIMALS, CLASSIFICATION OF; SILICON

Porosity Porosity is the characteristic of being *porous,* or filled with tiny holes through which water, air, or the like pass. Sponges and sandstone are porous. VIRUSES can pass through pores in porcelain filters.

Porpoise

Porpoise (POR-puss) Both porpoises and DOLPHINS belong in the same group called *cetaceans* (large sea animals). They are MAMMALS that usually live in seawater. While they are fish-like in shape, they have horizontal tails or *flukes* instead of vertical ones. Like whales, porpoises breathe air through lungs and expel it through a blowhole on the top of the head. Moisture in the warm air condenses and they seem to spout a stream of water from the blow-hole.

Two species live in America's coastal waters. The blunt-nosed harbor species are quite similar. One lives in the Atlantic and the other in the Pacific. Both are about 6 feet (1.8 meters) long and weigh around 100 pounds (45 kilograms). They have black backs, a triangular dorsal fin, pink-tinted sides, and white bellies. Pectoral or ventral flippers are present, but fishlike pelvic or anal appendages are absent. The *Dall* porpoise has white on its belly and sides.

Porpoises swim near the surface of the water in schools of 50 to 75, following the leader. If the leader heads for a beach, the whole school will become stranded.

All porpoises have about 27 sharp, spade-shaped teeth along each side of each jaw. They feed on fish and squid and will travel great distances in search of food.

Calves, about 30 to 35 inches (76 to 89 centimeters) long, are born in the spring. A newborn is nursed by its mother as it swims at her side. J.C.K.

SEE ALSO: CETACEA, DOLPHIN, MAMMALIA, WHALE

Porter, Rodney R. (1917-) He is a British biochemist who shared in the 1972 NOBEL PRIZE in physiology and medicine. His research dealt with the basic structure of ANTIBODIES and how they fight disease.

Dr. Porter, and his co-winner Dr. Gerald M. Edelman, had independently investigated the structure of antibodies, substances that combat bacterial toxins and other foreign matter than can invade animals. They inspired co-workers to further the study of immunology and its practical applications. P.P.S.

Portuguese man-of-war see Man-of-War, Portuguese

Portulaca (pohr-tchuh-LACK-uh) Portulaca is an interesting small herb or flower. A native of Brazil, this little flower grows where nothing else will. It thrives in hot, dry, almost impossible places. Portulaca is also called *rose moss* for its low showy flowers.

Portulaca grows close to the ground, seldom reaching over 1 foot (.3 meter) in height. It has narrow, fleshy leaves and brightly colored flowers. They may be white, red, pink, yellow, or purple.

A garden variety of portulaca is used as a cooking herb. It grows to 1½ feet (.5 meter) tall, has bright yellow flowers and leaves ½ inch (1.3 centimeters) wide. J.K.K.

Positron (PAHZ-uh-trahn) Positrons (*elementary particles*) are ELECTRON *antiparticles* (electrons with positive electric charges). Dirac, from his study of the conservation laws, predicted in 1928 the existence of positrons. In 1932, C. D. Anderson, working at the California Institute, found positrons in his experiments. He named the positron for its *posi*tive charge and its similarity to the elec*tron*.

Positrons are emitted from a nucleus by a *proton* changing into a *neutron* inside the nucleus of an atom. Such a change occurs spontaneously in many radioactive elements. The positron can combine with a free ELECTRON and the two disappear by forming two gamma rays. This is called *pair annihilation* because the electrons and positrons disappear. In the absence of electrons (in vacuum), the positron is stable and can live forever. In the presence of matter, such as most solids, the positron lives a very short time (one billionth of a second).

Positrons were predicated theoretically, before their experimental discovery, by the English physicist P. A. M. Dirac. In Dirac's theory, negative energies for electrons exist as well as the ordinary positive energies. A positron comes into existence when an electron is removed from the region of filled negative energy states. The "hole" left by the electron is the positron. To form such a hole, energy must be put into the region. When a PHOTON is absorbed in the vicinity of a charged particle, one negative electron and one positive positron are created. This process is called *pair production*. J. K. L.

Posterior Posterior means the hind or tail end (*caudal*) on most animals. In upright animals, posterior refers to the back or dorsal side.

SEE: ANIMALS, CLASSIFICATION OF

Posture To have good posture should be one of the most important health goals. With head held high and shoulders level, a person will feel better. Standing correctly helps the blood move freely to the brain and circulate better throughout the body. The organs with which people breathe, digest food, and get rid of waste materials do their best work when in their proper position.

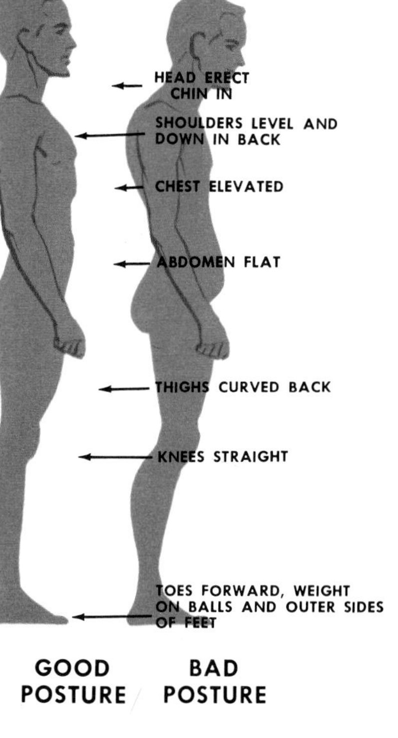

Potash Potash is a name often used for a chemical known as *potassium carbonate.* This chemical was originally obtained from wood ashes and thereby received its name. Potash is used in the manufacture of soaps and glass.

Potassium carbonate is very soluble in water, and the solution that results is alkaline. In its dry or *anhydrous* form, it takes up water very readily even from the air itself. For this reason it is used to remove water from organic liquids when the water is not wanted.

In its pure dry form, potash is a white, odorless, granular powder. Its chemical formula is K_2CO_3. Its molecular weight is 138.2. M. S.

Potassium (puh-TASS-ee-um) Potassium is one of the alkali metals and the 19th element. It was first prepared in the pure form by SIR HUMPHRY DAVY in 1808. It appears as a soft silvery-white metal when pure. In the form of various minerals and salts, it makes up 2.4% of the earth's crust.

Potassium is one of the most active metals known. It reacts with the oxygen in the air and very vigorously with water. In order to keep potassium from reacting in storage, it must be immersed in a liquid that does not contain oxygen, such as petroleum or other liquid hydrocarbons.

Its main uses are in chemical reactions to make other compounds or salts containing potassium. Some of the more familiar compounds and their uses are as follows: potassium *bicarbonate* in baking powders; potassium *bromide* as a sedative; potassium *carbonate* (potash) in soap manufacturing; potassium *chlorate* in fireworks and EXPLOSIVES; potassium *chloride* in medicine; potassium *dichromate* in leather tanning; potassium *ferrocyanide* in dyeing wool and silk; potassium *hydroxide* in soap manufacturing; potassium *iodide* in analytical chemistry; potassium *nitrate* in gunpowder; potassium *oleate,* a soap; potassium *permanganate,* an antiseptic; potassium *persulfate* for bleaching fabrics; potassium *sulfite* in photographic developers.

Potassium (symbol K from Latin *Kalium*) has atomic weight 39.102.

Recently, potassium has become important in dating materials that are older than the carbon-14 method can date. A very active ISOTOPE of potassium, K^{40} slowly but steadily changes into argon-40. For example, it would take 1 3/10 billion years for half of 18 K^{40} atoms to decay to argon-40. The time is long but it can be calculated from the number of K^{40} atoms remaining. The discovery that man may be one million years older than previously thought is the result of such calculation. M. S.

SEE ALSO: ELEMENTS, ELEMENTS IN THE HUMAN BODY, NUCLEAR SCIENCE

Potato This flowering plant grows to be from 2 to 4 feet (.6 to 1.2 meters) tall. It is grown in northern climates as an annual. In southern climates, it will live for several years. It has stems above and below the soil. The underground stem is a vegetable.

Potato LEAVES are pinnately compound. It has spreading stalks and dark green leaves. FLOWERS are small and white, lavender, blue, or yellow, depending upon the variety. Petals form a tube-shaped bloom. The small FRUIT is a berry that looks like a tiny green or purple tomato, a relative. Each contains a few to several hundred seeds.

The potato has a fibrous ROOT system. The underground *stolon* (stem) produces swollen *tubers,* which are eaten. It is thought that a fungus initiates tuberization. Potatoes are about 78 percent water, 18 percent carbohydrates, and 4 percent proteins, minerals, and fats. Enemies of potato include blight fungus, bacterial rot, and the potato beetle.

The Solanaceae family is commonly called the potato family. H. J. C.

SEE ALSO: TOMATO, VEGETABLE

Potential Potential is a measure of the amount of a stored quantity available for possible use. Potential ENERGY is energy of position. It is the work which has been done to put something in a potential where it is ready to move due to the presence of some force. This force may be gravitational, mechanical, electrical, magnetic, etc.

Potentilla

Potentilla (poh-tuhn-TILL-uh) This is the name for about 300 kinds of HERBS. They grow wild on lawns and prairies in the eastern United States. Some of these herbs are also called *cinquefoil* because each leaf is divided into five parts. A few kinds develop runners with three-part leaves.

Poultry see Chicken, Fowl

Pound see Foot-pound, Measurement

Powell, Cecil Frank (1903-1969) The 1950 NOBEL PRIZE in physics was awarded to an English nuclear physicist, Cecil Powell. He was responsible for the discovery in 1947 of two new particles, the *pi-meson* and the *mu-meson.*

With his co-workers, he devised a technique for photographing the tracks of particles. They obtained photographic evidence of the pi-meson and the mu-meson. They also determined the modes of decay for these particles. A.J.H.

Power Power depends upon how fast work is done. WORK is done whenever a push or pull moves something. The work may be done slowly or quickly. If work is done quickly, greater power is expended than when it is done slowly.

The push or pull needed to move something is called *force* and the work done is the force times the distance the object is moved. Power $=\frac{\text{WORK}}{\text{TIME}}$. If a boy weighing 80 pounds (36 kilograms) climbs 20 feet (6 meters) up a ladder, 1600 ft-lbs (2169 joules) of work is done against gravity. The force the boy needs to climb the ladder equals his own weight. If the boy climbs the ladder in 4 seconds, the power equals 1600 ft-lbs ÷ 4 sec., or 400 ft-lbs per second (or 2169 joules ÷ 4 seconds = 542 watts). If he takes 8 seconds to climb, the power is less. The power then equals 200 ft-lbs per second (270 watts). Thus, power is the time rate of doing work.

Power may be expressed in many different units, such as *horsepower, watts,* or *joules per second.* The watt rating on an electric light bulb gives the rate at which electrical energy (work) will be consumed when the bulb is used. The 100 watts means 100 joules per second. This is a unit of power MEASUREMENT in the metric system. J.H.D.

SEE ALSO: ENERGY; MACHINES, SIMPLE

Prairie A prairie is an open tract of land where the climax or index plants are grasses. This stable natural community once covered a large area of the middle part of North America. Much of the natural prairie has been cultivated for crops or used as pasture for livestock.

The temperature, soil, and the amount of rainfall determine if an area is suitable for grasses. They require a soil rich in humus. A root system may extend 12 feet (4 meters) into the ground. Regions that have prolonged droughts and less than 10 inches (25 centimeters) of annual rain are not good for a prairie. It takes over 30 inches (75 centimeters) of rain each year to support a forest.

Life was once abundant in the original prairie BIOME. The harvester ants, locusts, and wasps found their niches with the prairie dog, jumping mice, and pocket gophers. Pronghorned antelope, bobcats, and coyotes ran through the big bluestem, Indian grass, and Canadian wild rye. The bobolinks, meadow larks, and plovers found food and nesting places in wheatgrass, grana, and buffalograss. The prairie was a blaze of color from early spring to late fall with such forbs as shooting stars, Indian paintbrush, butterfly weed, snakeroot, wild hyacinth, asters, and sunflowers.

Prairies are vast open areas with few trees

Courtesy Society For Visual Education, Inc.

Only traces of native prairie remain today. The prairie chicken, wild horse, and bison are gone. Conservationists are attempting to preserve the few natural prairies remaining. Nature centers are developing prairie restoration sites from seeds gathered along unplowed railroad tracts. However, restoring the animal population is impossible. The grasslands now serve people instead of the wide diversity of living things it once did. H.J.C.

Prairie chicken see Grouse

Prairie dog The prairie dog is a small, wild rodent with very short ears and a short, flat tail with a black tip. This stout, sturdy animal is about 15 inches (38 centimeters) long, and has coarse brownish fur with some gray and black hairs. Prairie dogs like high dry prairies. They are found from Texas and Kansas to the Rocky Mountains, and north to Montana.

Prairie dogs live in large colonies. Their underground burrows are very cleverly constructed and may cover many miles. Each opening into the burrows has a mound of earth around it to prevent rain water from running in. The prairie dog will sit in the opening like a guard and watch for danger. In case of danger, it sounds a shrill alarm and quickly ducks into the burrow. Just inside the burrow entrance are rooms where it goes to listen for the danger to pass. Farther down in the burrow are many passages and rooms. Some are lined with grass for care of the young. Prairie dogs live on grasses, weeds, and some insects. M.R.L.

SEE ALSO: RODENTIA

Prairie wolf see Coyote

Praseodymium (pray-see-oh-DIMM-ee-uhm) Praseodymium is RARE-EARTH ELEMENT 59 in MENDELEEV'S PERIODIC TABLE. It is in *cerite* and other rare minerals. Its symbol is Pr. Its atomic number is 59 and atomic weight is 140.907. It is naturally silvery white but its salts are green.

Its common oxide (Pr_6O_{11}) is a black powder. The salts of praseodymium are produced by dissolving the black oxide in an acid. These salts are used in the ceramic industry for glazes and coloring glass.

Von Welsbach discovered the element in 1885 when he separated the salts of didymium into praseodymium and NEODYMIUM. E. R. B.

SEE ALSO: ELEMENTS, OXIDATION

Courtesy Society For Visual Education, Inc.

A mantis searching for prey

Praying mantis The mantis or *mantid* is an insect that has long, folding front legs. It usually sits on a plant with these legs poised ready to snatch another passing insect for its prey. This posture reminded early naturalists of a human attitude of prayer, and thus suggested the name. The mantis is actually harmless to large animals and is valuable because it eats grasshoppers and other insect pests. Most species live in the tropics, but the American and common European species live well north. The European species is becoming common as an imported species in the United States.

The mantis is a cannibal, for it eats other mantises as well as other insects. The female often eats its own mate.

Related to the grasshoppers, crickets, and cockroaches, the mantis is slender with long legs, oval wings, a long neck or *prothora,* and an angular movable head with large, protruding eyes. The front legs are stout, spiny, and fitted for seizing their prey like a spring trap. Mantises are 2 to 5 inches (5 to 13 centimeters) long. They resemble the leaves of plants. J.K.K.

SEE ALSO: INSECTA

Pre-Cambrian see Geologic time table

Precious stones see Gem

✳ THINGS TO DO

HOW TO MAKE A PRECIPITATE WITH LIMEWATER TABLETS

Materials: Limewater tablets (from drugstore), 2 tumblers or test tubes, funnel, filter paper, soda water, straw

1. **Dissolve 1 or 2 small limewater tablets in a tumbler of cold water. Keep weak lime solution off of skin.**
2. **Filter the milky solution with a funnel lined with filter paper. Do this within ½ hour, since carbon dioxide of the air will recloud the clear liquid coming through filter.**
3. **Divide the resulting clear limewater into two portions. To one, add a little fresh carbonated water. The white precipitate formed is calcium carbonate.**
4. **Show that your breath also contains carbon dioxide that will make lime carbonate precipitate. Simply blow with a soda straw into the weak, clear limewater.**

Note: If you breathe too long, the white carbonate will redissolve. This is because it forms soluble, non-precipitated calcium hydrogen (bi-) carbonate. **D. A. B.**

Precipitation (chemical) (pruh-SIPP-ih-tay-shunn) When some specific chemical is added to a solution, a solid mass of new chemical is often formed. This solid material is the result of a reaction between the solution and the chemical which has been added to it. The new, insoluble substance is a *precipitate;* and the process by which it forms is called *precipitation.*

Two common examples of precipitation are: (1) the formation of a white, finely-divided cloudy mass (*calcium carbonate*) when a person blows his breath (with *carbon dioxide* in it) into clear *limewater*; (2) the formation of a white scum (which in most hard waters is *lime-* and *magnesium-soap salts*) when soap is mixed with hard water.

Four conditions or factors affect precipitation: (1) the solubility of both original and newly formed chemicals in a given reaction; (2) the particular concentration of chemicals—including *ions,* if any—in the mixture being studied; (3) the temperature of the mixture; (4) the chemical nature (*chemical equation*) of the mixture being studied. Other factors important in some complex precipitations include (a) the effect of *super-saturation,* and (b) the law of *mass action,* which is a mathematical rule concerning the strength of each type of *molecule,* or ion, in the reacting solution.

Certain changes in complex *colloidal* solutions seem to be precipitations but actually are not. For example, when clear egg white is cooked to a white solid or when milk curdles, the change is a molecule-clumping one, called *coagulation*—not true precipitation. Again, when a solution is merely heated to remove water and obtain a solid residue, that process is *separation by evaporation.*

Precipitation is widely used in chemistry. It finds its two most important uses, first, in the identification of chemicals in mixtures of unknown composition, and, second, in the separation of certain chemicals into a pure, solidified form from their natural or processed mixtures. D. A. B.

SEE ALSO: CHEMISTRY

✳ **THINGS TO DO**

WHERE DOES RAIN COME FROM?

1. **Place a wooden flat of grass on a table near a kettle of boiling water. Hold a pan of ice cubes or crushed ice over the spout. As the steam hits the cold bottom of the pan droplets of water will form. As the drops increase in size they will fall on the grass as rain.**
2. **The warm air coming from the teakettle is laden with water vapor. As it hits the cold surface it must condense some to liquid water. Cool air cannot hold as much moisture as warm air.**

Precipitation (weather) (pruh-SIPP-ih-TAY-shunn) In meteorology, the scientific study of weather, the term precipitation means the falling of moisture from clouds to the surface of the earth. Only four forms of falling water are classified as precipitation. They are rain, snow, sleet, and hail. Meteorologists do not consider dew and frost to be forms of precipitation.

Precipitation is one of the three steps in the continuous *water cycle*. The other two steps are evaporation and condensation. Oceans and other water bodies release moisture into the atmosphere in the form of *water vapor*. This is called evaporation. As water vapor is cooled in the atmosphere, it condenses into liquid water and forms clouds. Two conditions must be present for water vapor to condense. First, there must be sufficient cooling for the molecules of water vapor to move closer together. Second, there must be dust particles in the air around which the water molecules can condense. The particles serve as *condensation nuclei*. Condensation is the process that changes the state of water from gaseous to liquid form.

Condensation does not necessarily produce precipitation. Cooling within the atmosphere causes vapor condensation and formation of clouds. The clouds are made up of droplets of liquid water, that are so small and light that they remain suspended in the air. If further cooling takes place within the cloud, the tiny droplets join together to form larger, heavier drops that fall as rain. If temperatures are below freezing in the area of cloud formation, water vapor changes directly into the solid form (*sublimation*), and snow crystals are the result.

In the winter, temperature *inversions* may form in the layers of the air. The layers at or near the ground are below freezing; warmer rain cloud layers are above. As raindrops fall through the freezing layers, they become small pellets of clear ice called *sleet*.

Hail is not the same as sleet. Sleet occurs mostly in the winter; hail is most often associated with summer thunderstorms. Such storms are composed of giant convectional currents that force large amounts of air both upward and downward. Raindrops falling in this area may be caught up by a rising current and swept into areas that are below freezing. The drops freeze. The ice particles then fall back into areas of heavy rain where they acquire an additional coating of water. They may then be forced to rise again, and the new coating of water also freezes. The more round trips the hailstones make, the larger they become.

In order for precipitation of any type to occur, cooling must take place. Cooling is most frequently the result of air being forced to rise in some manner that causes *adiabatic* cooling within the air. Air may be forced to rise by convectional currents, by passing over mountains, or by frontal activity during which cold, dense air displaces warmer air in an upward direction.

Of the four forms of falling precipitation, only rain and snow are measured. The amount of snowfall is converted into equivalent inches (centimeters) of rain by melting the snow and pouring it into a rain gauge. This measurement is added to the actual rainfall to give total precipitation for the year H.S.G.

SEE ALSO: CLOUDS, RAINMAKING, WEATHER

Predator-prey This is a relationship between two animals. One animal is attacked, killed, and usually eaten as food by another.

A snake is a predator that preys upon

frogs. A hydra attacks daphnia. A fox hunts squirrels. Man is the prey of a tapeworm. In a stable ECOSYSTEM the natural predator-prey relationship keeps all populations in balance. People trying to control predators often seriously upset this natural balance.

Predation is a significant factor in evolution. The sick, hurt, or weak members of a species are the ones most often killed. This leaves the healthy and strong to reproduce.

The top predator in a food pyramid is usually not a prey. Their population is controlled by disease, lack of food, old age, or hunters. H.J.C.

SEE ALSO: BALANCE OF NATURE

Pregnancy Pregnancy is the period during which a baby is contained in its mother's uterus, or womb, before it is born. Human pregnancy lasts about nine months; during this time the baby grows from a tiny fertilized egg to a baby.

First signs of pregnancy are cessation of MENSTRUATION, enlargement of the breast, and other bodily changes, and sometimes a kind of *nausea* called "morning sickness."

Pregnancy begins at *conception* when the *sperm* fertilizes the *ovum.* The fertilized ovum sends out little threadlike *villi* which attach themselves to the wall of the *uterus* and grow to become the fetal portion of the *placenta.* The placenta is a special structure of glands and blood vessels through which the baby receives nourishment.

By the end of the fourth month, the mother feels "signs of life," the restless movements of the baby, or *fetus,* and the doctor can distinguish the fetal heartbeat.

Pregnancy ends with *labor,* the process by which the baby is expelled from the uterus and given BIRTH to or *born.* J. M. C.

SEE ALSO: GESTATION PERIOD; REPRODUCTION, SEXUAL

Pregl, Fritz (1869-1930) Fritz Pregl, an Austrian scientist, was awarded the 1923 NOBEL PRIZE in chemistry. He developed micromethods for determining very small quantities of substances in biological materials.

Between 1910 and 1913 he developed microtechniques of quantitative analysis. He then spent the rest of his career perfecting the methods of determining amounts of hydrogen, nitrogen, oxygen, carbon, and organic groups in biological specimens. He is considered the founder of microchemical analysis. A.J.H.

Prehensile Prehensile means able to seize or grasp by coiling around and clinging to an object. It is illustrated by the folding of the fingers around an object in the palm, or by the action of a MONKEY'S tail.

Prehistoric mammals Mammals first appeared on Earth during the Mesozoic Era (the Era of Reptiles). They were small, warm-blooded animals with hair, that looked very much like the reptiles from which they descended. Toward the end of the MESOZOIC ERA, the earth and its climate gradually began to change. The climate became colder and the swamplands, covered with thick green vegetation, began to disappear.

Over a period of thousands of years, mammals gradually developed which were able to survive in these new surroundings. Their warm blood and hair protected them from the cold. Their larger brains and ability to move quickly made it possible for them to escape from enemies and to catch food. They developed special teeth and more efficient digestive systems. Instead of laying their eggs on the ground and forgetting about them as the dinosaurs did, they were live-bearing animals which carried their fertilized eggs inside of their bodies until they had developed into baby animals. After their babies were born, they fed and cared for them until the young animals were able to take care of themselves. These changes made it possible for more mammals to survive.

Chicago Natural History Museum

Moropus, a prehistoric relative of the horse

A four-toed prehistoric horse

During the end of the Mesozoic Era and the beginning of the CENOZOIC ERA, the period in which man now lives, the ancestors of modern mammals, such as the HORSE, CAMEL, and BEAR, appeared on earth. The first camel, the *Protylopus,* looked like a baby goat. The flesh-eating (carnivorous) mammals, called *Creodonts,* looked like weasels. The *Miacis* was one of these early carnivores. The *Barylambda,* an ancient animal 8 feet (2.4 meters) long, ate both plants and small animals.

The Cenozoic Era (Era of Mammals) followed the Mesozoic Era (Era of Reptiles). During the middle of the Cenozoic Era, there appeared dog- and cat-like animals. The *Hyaenodon,* a hyena-like animal, lived during this time. Later in the era the ancestors of the ELEPHANT developed. During the Ice Age, less than one million years ago, *wooly* MAMMOTHS and MASTODONS roamed the ice-covered lands. Early camels, *llamas,* one-toed horses, and *giant ground sloths* wandered over the plains.

Some present-day mammals, such as the *opossum* and *rhinoceros,* look very much like their prehistoric ancestors. Others, such as the horse and elephant, look very different.

Ancestors of modern man were prehistoric mammals. Fossil remains of these primates have been found in Asia, Africa, China and Java. Fragments of skeletons plus artifacts show the gradual change which was taking place in his form and structure. The body was erect but posture poor; the brain was larger than in lower mammals; the teeth were more even. The chin developed and the nose became smaller. As each year passes, the prehistoric story becomes more complete.

The horse family began with a small horse the size of a fox. It was called the *dawn horse* (*Eohippus* or *Hyracotherium*). It had a few stiff hairs (instead of a mane), a small tail, and short neck. It had four toes on its front feet and three on its hind feet. After thousands of years the dawn horse developed into a three-toed horse known as the *middle horse* (*Mesohippus.*) About the same time, there lived a similar animal called a *Moropus* that developed claws instead of hoofs. Over the years, horses grew larger and larger. Their three toes gradually evolved into one toe which became a hoof.

The elephant family began with a small piglike animal with two large front teeth. It was called a *Moeritherium.* As its descendants grew bigger, they developed longer legs, and necks, tusks, and a trunk. The *Palaeomastodon* stood 3 feet (.9 meter) tall and had a short trunk and short tusks. The elephant family continued to change for millions of years.

Other Ice Age mammals included the *giant ground sloth (Megatherium),* a plant-eating beast with a heavy body, a large thick tail, strong legs and huge curved claws; the *Glyptodon,* a huge armadillo-like animal with a spiked tail and a suit of armor; the *Irish elk,* which had antlers 7 to 8 feet (2.1 to 2.4 meters) wide; and shaggy-coated *ancient bison.* Many of these large mammals died out as the earth changed. Others developed into the mammals known today. D.J.A.

SEE ALSO: EVOLUTION, PALEONTOLOGY

Prehistoric man see Evolution of man, Stone Age

Prelog, Vladimir (1906-) The 1975 NOBEL PRIZE in chemistry was awarded to Vladimir Prelog and John W. Cornforth. Prelog, an organic chemist, did important research in the field of stereochemistry.

Stereochemistry is the study of how organic compounds are affected by the spatial arrangement of their atoms. Prelog and his associates devised a system for naming organic compounds according to their structural configurations. A.J.H.

Presbyopia see Optometry

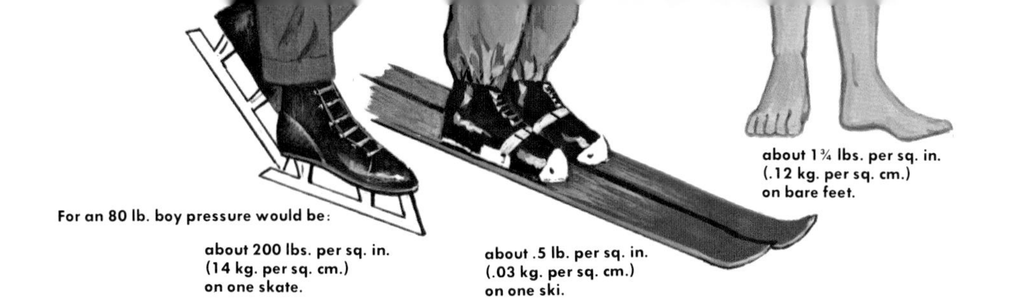

The pressure exerted by an object on a surface depends in part on the size of the object

Prescription see Drugs

Preserve A preserve is an area of land set aside to protect plants and animals. Preserves represent an attempt to restore the balance of nature in an area. They may be established by private, local, state, or federal organizations.

The establishment of preserves is a conservation method for living things. Forest and game preserves are continually being organized. They take constant observation and management. Preserves serve many valuable purposes. They are living libraries for children. Specialists in biology use them as laboratories for research and study. Nature centers can be used as outdoor teaching areas.

Both private organizations as well as governments operate preserves in North America. The National Audubon Society owns and manages hundreds of sanctuaries. The U.S. Forest Service administers 187 million acres (75.7 million hectares) of forest land. The U.S. Fish and Wildlife Service has 30 million acres (12 million hectares) of land to manage. Canada has set aside 50,000 square miles (130,000 square kilometers) for its 70 national parks.

The Wilderness Act of 1964 and the Land and Water Conservation Fund Act of 1965 are examples of federal legislation designed to maintain natural land. H. J. C.

Florida Swamp Harold Hungerford

Pressure Pressure is the force (or push) on some area of an object. Pressure is often measured in pounds per square inch or kilograms per square centimeter. For example, pressure of the air at SEA LEVEL is about 14.7 pounds per square inch (1.03 kilograms per square centimeter).

Pressure may be produced by solids, liquids, and gases. When a person dives under water, the pressure on the body is greater than AIR PRESSURE because the weight of the water above exerts pressure too. When a boy or girl skates on ice, the pressure under the runner of the skates is very great because of the weight of the body on the small area of the runner.

In a LIQUID, pressure is transmitted equally in all directions. The pressure in a liquid depends upon the height (depth) and the density of the liquid. The pressure (p) at any depth (h) for a liquid density (d) is given by the formula: $p = d \times h$.

Pressure causes gases to expand and contract. This scientific fact has led to the development of air tires and air brakes.

The United States Weather Bureau report air pressure on the daily weather maps. Air pressure changes occur before storms.

In the metric system, pressure may be expressed in many different units such as grams per square centimeter, dynes per square centimeter, and bars or millibars. A bar is 1,000,000 dynes per square centimeter. J.H.D.

SEE ALSO: BAROMETER, GAS, HYDRAULICS, MEASUREMENT, WEATHER.

Pressure gauge A pressure gauge measures PRESSURE, the force which acts evenly upon a unit area. Usually a pressure gauge consists of a metal tube or diaphragm which bends as the pressure varies. An attached hand acts as a pointer against a scale.

SEE: BAROMETER, MANOMETER

Prickly heat Prickly heat is a red, pimply rash located around sweat glands (such as under the arms). It occurs when a person becomes overheated and perspires a lot. It can be very itchy, and can become infected if scratched.

Prickly pear see Cactus

Priestley, Joseph (1733-1804) Though Joseph Priestley is primarily known as the English clergyman who discovered oxygen, he was a man with many talents. Priestley was awarded a doctor of law degree from the University of Edinburgh for an essay on education and for writing biographies of important men through the ages. At Benjamin Franklin's request, Priestley wrote a *History of Electricity,* which was so successful that Priestley was asked to be a member of the Royal Society.

In 1767, after disagreeing with the trustees of the school in Warrington, Priestley resigned his teaching post and became the pastor of a small chapel near Leeds. Living next door to a brewery, he became interested in the "fixed air" (carbon dioxide), which hung above the liquid in the large fermentation vats. Soon he moved to another location, and there he successfully made carbon dioxide by pouring acid on chalk. Then he dissolved the gas in water and obtained carbonated water.

In 1774, Priestley obtained a new gas from mercuric oxide that he called a new kind of air. He suggested that it might be used to aid breathing in certain instances, and this suggestion proved to be the forerunner of oxygen tents.

This discovery of a new gas brought Priestley even more fame and led to a meeting with ANTOINE LAVOISIER and other important scientists in Paris. Lavoisier immediately repeated Priestley's experiments with the new gas, and then named the gas *oxygen* because of its acid-forming properties. D. H. J.

Primary color see Color

Primates (PRY-mahts) Primates are the group of mammals of which man is a member. Many primates walk uprightly or semi-uprightly. They live in warm regions. The primates include the monkey and similar animals. They often live as families within groups.

Primates are generally distinguished from other mammals in several respects. The nervous systems tend to be more highly developed. The brain case is larger. Primates have "hand-like" parts and flat walking feet. Nails, at least on some digits, instead of claws are typical. The two eyes surrounded by a bony ring, are aimed frontward, and focus on the same object. This ability promotes distance perception, a valuable adaptation to tree-swinging animals.

There are eight families among the primates. Animals representative of each are as follows, with the scientific family name in parentheses:

Aye-Aye (*Chiranyidae*): This cat-sized animal has a long bushy tail and claws on its back feet except the flat-nailed big toe. Aye-Ayes live in Madagascar.

Lemur (*Lemuridae*): This squirrel-sized animal is quite unlike other primates except for the feet. There are many kinds of lemurs, some very peculiar looking, especially the loris. *Lemur* means "ghost." They are found principally in Madagascar.

Tarsier (*Tarsiidae*): These are among the most primitive primates. They have big staring eyes, long ankles, and jump like frogs. They are rat-sized, living in the East Indies.

Marmoset (*Hapalidae*): These small primates have prehensile tails and resemble monkeys. They are natives of Central and South America.

Baboon (*Cercopithecidae*): This is one of the Old World monkeys. They typically have nostrils close together, directed downwards. They have heavy-skinned sitting areas. The face is dog-like.

Capuchin monkey (*Cebidae*): Of many New World monkeys, the Capuchin is popularized as the organ grinder's monkey. Animals of this group are smallish with opposable thumbs and great toes. They have long prehensile tails and widely-spaced, side opening nostrils.

These baboons have the dog-like faces common to their family.

The primate family ranges from the primitive lemurs and tarsiers to man.

Manlike apes (*Simiidae*)*:* These are the anthropoid apes, or manlike apes, man's closest animal kin. All probably had a common ancestor as, similarly, would dogs, cats, lions, and wolves. The *anthropoids* (manlike) are larger than monkeys, possessing larger brains.

Four main anthropoid types are the long-armed *gibbon;* the reddish-haired *orangutan;* appealing *chimpanzee* (easiest to train to amusing human ways); and the powerful *gorilla,* mentally less acute than the chimpanzees, and most ferocious. Gorillas are short-lived in captivity.

Anthropoids are skeletally like man. Ears are round and flat; unlike man's they are not lobed. They aren't completely upright creatures and cannot talk or use fire. They are more manlike than the monkeys.

Man (*Hominidae*): Man, *Homo sapiens,* has a brain twice that of the highest ape. He is a completely upright, two-footed walker. He is less hairy than other primates. His mental development has become his chief adaptation to living anywhere he desires; he is indeed "king of beasts." This advanced mentality has replaced physical adaptations and developments by which lower animals live successfully. D. J. I.

SEE ALSO: APE, CHIMPANZEE, EVOLUTION, EVOLUTION OF MAN, GIBBON, GORILLA, LEMUR, MAMMALIA, MONKEY, ORANGUTAN

Prime meridian see Time zones

Primrose The stem of the garden primrose is underground. A leafless flower stalk grows up from a circle of leaves. Flowers come in most colors and are tube or bell shaped. The fruit is a dry pod containing seeds.

There is also a family of plants called primrose (*Primulaceae*) that includes cyclamen. Many are native to England and Asia and are found in temperate regions of the United States. H. J. C.

Primroses

Helen Challand

Printed circuit A printed circuit is an electrical circuit that is made without the use of wires. It is usually made by imprinting a thin sheet of a non-conductor (such as plastic) with the circuit in a conducting material (such as copper).

Since printed circuits have no joints or other parts that can become loosened, they are very reliable; since they can be printed on flat sheets, they can be made very small. For these reasons they are used both commercially, as in TV sets, and in scientific instruments, as in space vehicles. D.A.B.

SEE ALSO: ELECTRONICS, TELEVISION

The basic process in printing is pressing one object against another

Printing Most school children have used a simple INK stamp to print pictures or words on paper. Sometimes stamps are made out of potatoes or sponges. Other stamps have letters of the alphabet formed out of rubber and attached to a wood or plastic handle. Ink is placed on the raised parts of the stamp. When the inked stamp is pressed against paper, an image appears. The stamp can be inked and pressed again, so that many nearly identical images are made.

Today there are many different methods of printing. Most are performed by pressing one object against another so that it leaves a mark.

HOW PRINTING BEGAN

Early people painted on rocks pictures of hunters and animals. In later civilizations, people learned to make symbols that represented certain spoken words. It was not until 25,000 years ago, however, that the Phoenicians finally worked out a system for writing individual sounds. From this discovery, they were able to invent the first alphabet. With an alphabet, spoken words could be accurately recorded.

The next problem was that of reproducing identical copies of words and pictures. The ancient Egyptians and Babylonians were the first to develop tools for printing. By carving symbols into wood or stone, they made small hand stamps. These were used for making prints in soft metal coins or clay pots. In fact, the Babylonians invented a tool for printing a complete paragraph. Letters were scratched around the surface of a wooden cylinder. An entire paragraph could be rolled onto a soft clay tablet with one turn of the cylinder.

People had not as yet learned how to make ink marks on paper. It was not until the 5th century A.D. that the Chinese began to use similar wooden stamps for making ink marks on paper. These small stamps were gradually replaced by blocks large enough to print a complete picture. After the block was carved, a damp sheet of paper, placed over the inked surface, was rubbed by hand until a print was made. So successful were the Chinese with wood blocks that they produced millions of copies of paper money.

THE INVENTION OF MOVABLE TYPE

When letters are formed separately, they may be grouped into words, sentences, and paragraphs. They may be taken apart and reassembled to form new words. Typewriters have movable type. The individual letters may be used in any combination.

Block printing was an important step to the invention of movable type. Although the individual letters could not be reused, the blocks produced identical ink prints. In the 11th century, the Chinese were again the first to print from movable type. They made individual letters out of baked clay, which were then assembled in a frame.

Pages and sample letters from the Gutenberg press with movable type

THE FIRST PRINTING PRESS

It is interesting to think that people wrote for almost 2,000 years before they learned how to print by machine. In the middle of the 15th century, a goldsmith from Germany, Johannes Gutenberg, put together the first workable press. Used originally for making wine, the press operated with a screw that brought together two flat surfaces. Each page of movable type, set by hand, was locked into a wooden frame, inked, and placed on the lower surface, or *press-bed.* After a sheet of paper was placed over the type, the upper surface was lowered by means of the screw. As the two surfaces came together, a print was made.

The press, which later became known as the *platen* or *flat bed press,* could produce about 300 pages a day. Although today this would amount to about three or four copies of one magazine, the speed output was superior to either handwriting or hand printing.

In 1883 the first cylinder press was developed. The type remained on a flat bed and the paper was placed on a cylinder. The cylinder moved from one end to the other, much like a rolling pin moves across dough.

The stereotype is a lightweight metal copy or mold of type that is on the surface of a cylinder. The type is set on a flat surface. A sheet of moist cardboard is placed over the type. Pressure is applied to the cardboard. The pressure forces an impression of the type into the cardboard. A thin layer of molten lead alloy is rolled over the cardboard mold to form sheets of type. The sheets of type are then bent to fit the curved cylindrical press. This led to the rotary press in which type and paper move over cylinders.

A machine called the linotype, which set and cast each line of type ready for printing, was patented in 1885. Finally, the camera was used in printing. Pictures were transferred by chemical means from photographic film to a metal printing plate.

ELECTROSTATIC PRINTING

In the dark, a pure silicon plate is a good

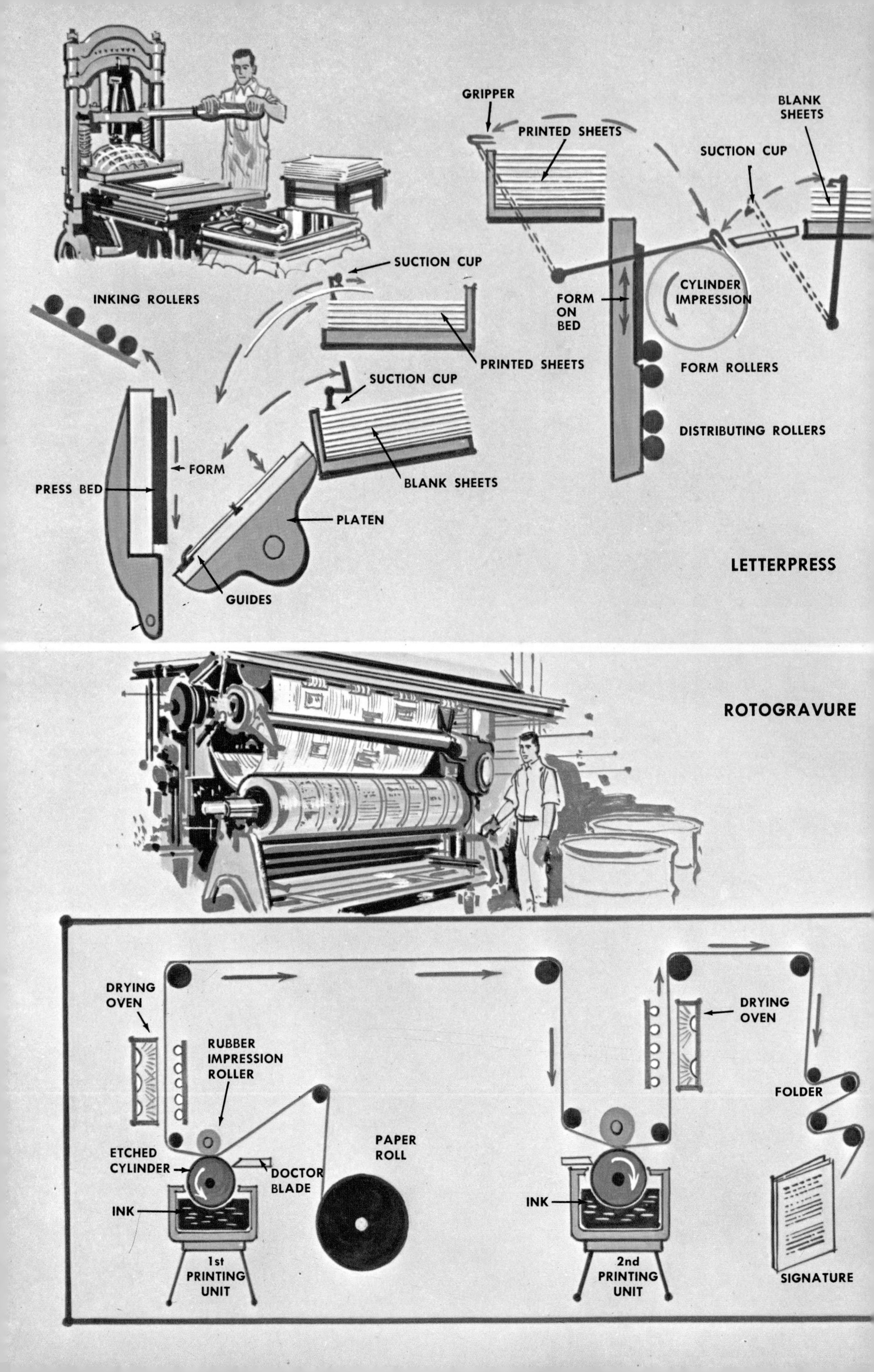
GRIPPER
PRINTED SHEETS
BLANK SHEETS
SUCTION CUP
SUCTION CUP
INKING ROLLERS
CYLINDER IMPRESSION
FORM ON BED
PRINTED SHEETS
FORM ROLLERS
SUCTION CUP
DISTRIBUTING ROLLERS
FORM
PRESS BED
BLANK SHEETS
PLATEN
LETTERPRESS
GUIDES
ROTOGRAVURE
DRYING OVEN
DRYING OVEN
RUBBER IMPRESSION ROLLER
FOLDER
PAPER ROLL
ETCHED CYLINDER
DOCTOR BLADE
INK
INK
1st PRINTING UNIT
2nd PRINTING UNIT
SIGNATURE

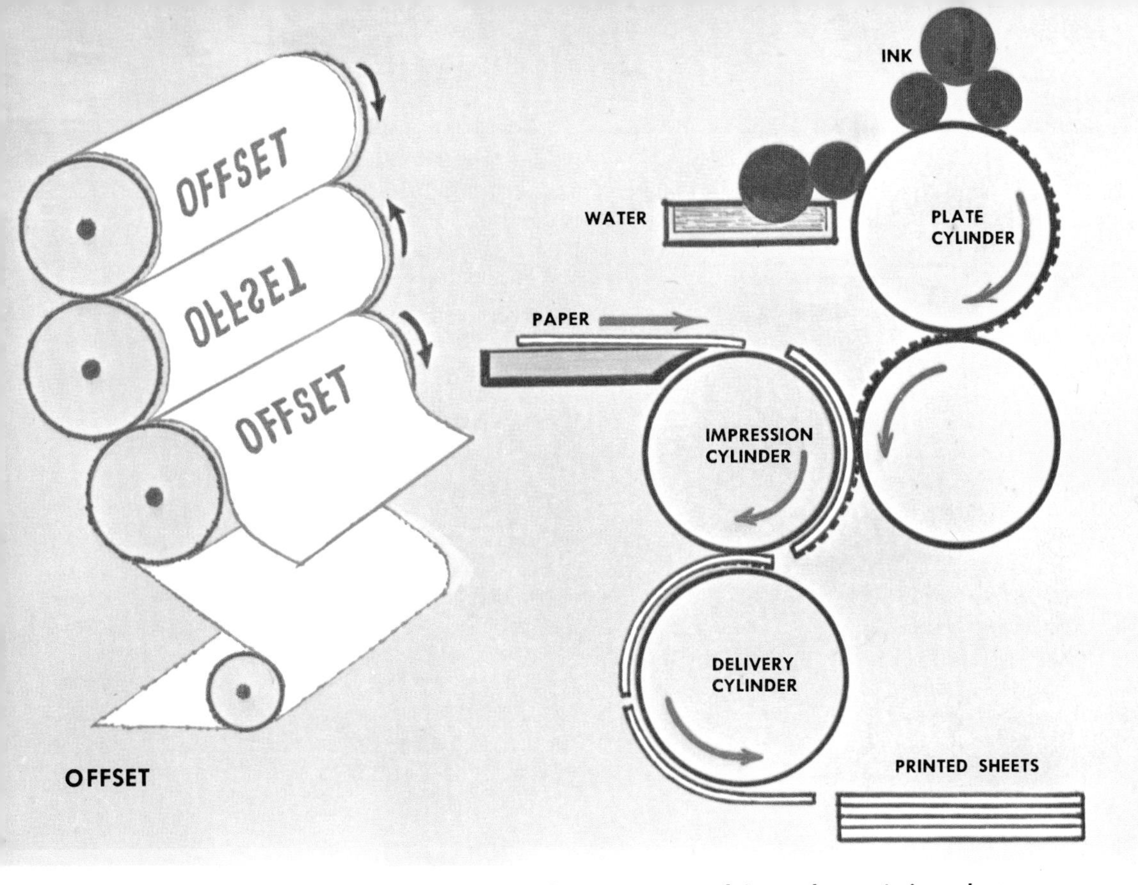

A large four-color offset lithography press as used in modern printing plants

Miehle Printing Press and Manufacturing Co.

insulation, and any charge on it will stay. When the plate is exposed to light, any charge on the plate will leak away.

A charged silicon plate that is exposed to a light and dark pattern, such as a printed page, develops an uneven charge. Only the shadowed sections caused by the letters hold the charge. When a black plastic powder is brushed over the plate, the letters hold the powder. If a charged sheet of paper contacts the plate, the powder will be transferred to the paper. When heated, powder and paper fuse to form a printed page.

RELIEF PRINTING

Since block printing is a type of relief printing, this is the oldest process. The principle is simple. Like letters on a typewriter, those parts of the plate which print are raised. Those that do not print are below the surface. A large volume of printed material is produced by this method, since it is used for printing newspapers, books, and magazines. Commercially it is known as *letterpress printing.*

When a black-and-white picture is to be printed, it is first photographed onto a negative and printed on a treated zinc plate, just as a picture is photographed on film and printed on paper. After being treated with chemicals, the parts that will not print are eaten away with acid, leaving those parts that will print raised.

But most pictures have light and dark shadows. In order to print accurately shaded areas, the *half-tone* process is used. One who examines newspaper photographs finds that they are made of tiny dots, smaller in light areas and larger in dark areas. The picture is photographed through a half-tone screen onto a treated metal plate. The screen consists of two sheets of glass, having parallel diagonal lines, filled with black pigment. These are placed face-to-face so that the lines are at right angles to one another, giving the effect of a window screen. The size of the dot varies with the amount of light striking the metal plate.

The most inexpensive color printing is the three-color process. Since any number of colors may be printed, the term is misleading. By making a separate plate for each color, the plates may be printed like the regular black-and-white plates. However, the colors are flat and less subtle than they are in other color processes.

The most expensive, but most accurate color printing, the *four-color process,* is similar to the half-tone process. The picture to be printed is photographed through color filters and half-tone screens to produce four separate colors—red, yellow, blue, and black. Thus, the printer has four dotted plates. By printing these on top of one another, practically any color may be made.

In letterpress printing, after copy and pictures are assembled, a stereotype, or copy, of the entire page is made. The giant *rotary presses* used by big city "dailies" have printing cylinders which carry 4 or 8 of these plates. Each time the cylinder turns, it will print 4 or 8 pages on one side of the paper and 4 or 8 on the other side. The continuous webs or rolls of paper are pressed against the printing cylinder by means of a second, or impression, cylinder. One press may contain several of these units. Each unit can produce about 50,000 impressions an hour. Smaller printing firms may use cylinder or *platen* presses.

PLANOGRAPHIC PRINTING

This method, one of the most recent, is based on the simple principle that grease and water will not mix. (Instead of being printed from a raised surface, both type and pictures are on a flat surface.)

Drawing or lettering was originally done on a thick porous stone with a crayon or ink mixed with tallow or wax. The surface of the stone was sponged with an acid, changing the surface not covered with wax into one which repelled grease and accepted water. The parts covered with wax accepted grease and repelled water. During printing, the stone was moistened with water, which soaked into those parts not drawn on. Printing ink, rolled over the surface, adhered only to the original drawing, which accepted ink.

Of course the heavy stone, still used in hand printing, is too awkward for commercial use. It has been replaced by a flexible, fine-textured *zinc* or *aluminum* plate. The image is photographed through a fine screen onto the plate. Since both text and pictures are printed from the same plate, the process is fast.

Commercially, planographic printing is called *offset lithography,* or *photo-offset.* Instead of printing directly on the paper, the metal plate prints on a rubber roller, which transfers the print to the paper. The elastic, rubber roller is able to pick up fine

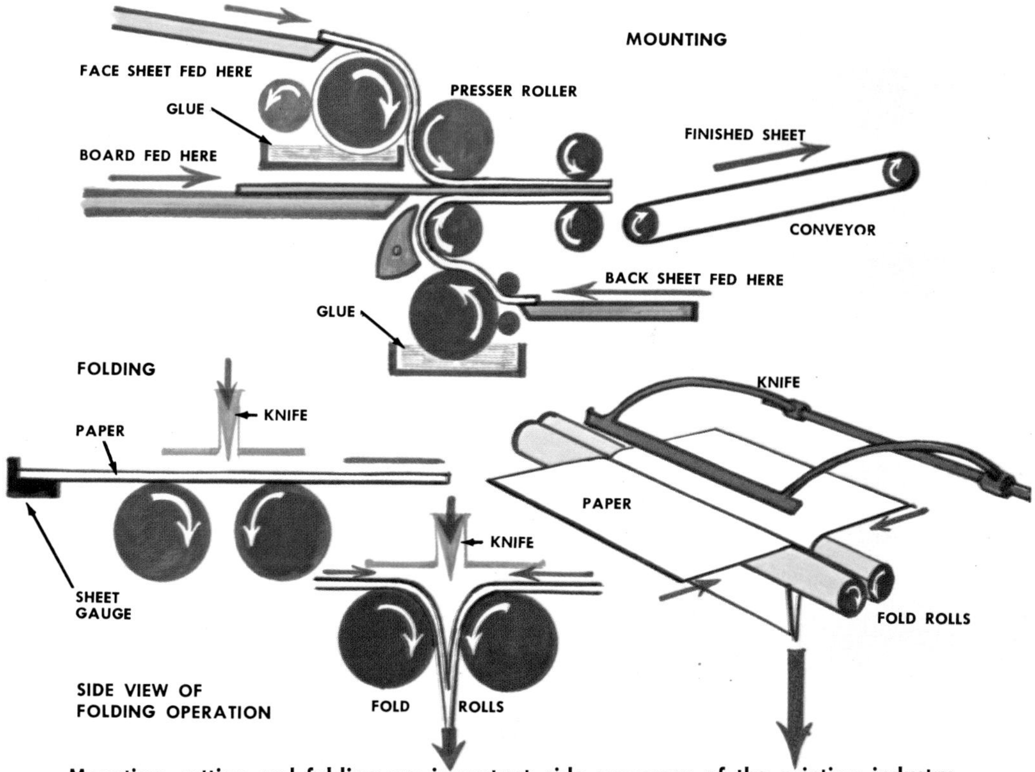

Mounting, cutting and folding are important side processes of the printing industry

dots and transfer them to rough paper, metal, wood, or canvas.

INTAGLIO PRINTING

In this process, both type and pictures are below the surface of the plate. Known before the time of Gutenberg, this method was called *engraving.* After the design or letters were cut into the steel or copper plate with a sharp V-shaped tool, the plate was covered with ink. Thus far, the process resembled block-printing. The entire surface wipes clean, however, so that the ink remained only in the lines. The plate, placed face down on a sheet of moist paper, was covered with felt and pressed with great pressure through a hand press. The ink was transferred to the paper by suction. The deeper the line, the darker the print.

Today this process is used for printing wedding invitations and certificates. The best known example is the printing of paper money and stamps by the Bureau of Engraving in Washington. The lines are severe, definite, and slightly raised.

Commercially, intaglio is known as *gravure printing—rotogravure* and *photogravure.* Pictures and words are reduced to small spots, which, instead of being raised above the surface as in relief printing, are small, square, microscopic wells below the surface. Although the cups are equal in size, they vary in depth. The deeper cups, which hold more ink, will transfer heavier deposits to the paper, thereby printing darker areas. Since the ink spreads over the paper, the dots overlap one another, giving a rich, velvety, slightly powdery quality. Big edition magazines, Sunday paper magazines and many high-quality art books are printed using the intaglio, or gravure printing, method.

COMPUTERS AND PRINTING

The rapid development of the electronic COMPUTER has revolutionized most aspects of the printing industry in recent decades. Small desktop and laptop computers are often used to write copy, which can then be delivered to remote typesetters on floppy disks or over phone lines. Typesetting equipment has been largely computerized since the 1960s. Even color art work can now be separated electronically by LASER scanners into the individual colors needed to make printing plates. By the 1990s, experiments using computerized scanners to make printing plates directly without film were well underway. Many modern printing presses are computer controlled as well.

The development in the 1980s of small, inexpensive laser printers made possible the phenomenon known as desktop publishing. By the early 1990s, the IBM and Hewlett-Packard companies had developed new laser printers, built around Japanese print engines, that produced print twice as sharp as the original, inexpensive laser printers. These printers were capable of producing printed words and line art that began to rival commercial black-and-white print quality, although half-tone photographs were not yet as sharp. E.P.L./J.H.

SEE ALSO: COMMUNICATION, COMPUTER, MACHINERY, PAPER, PHOTOGRAPHY

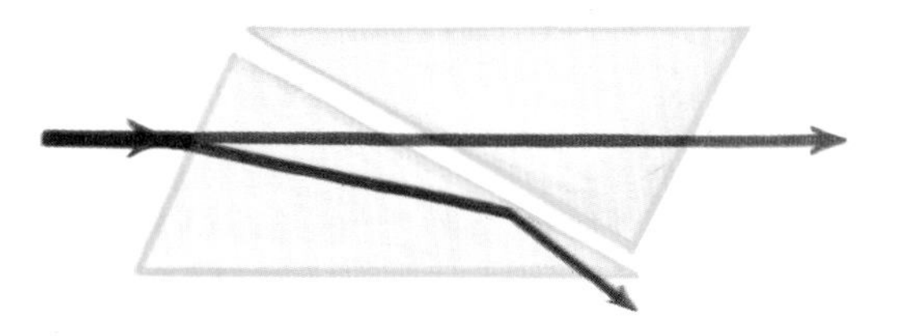

Polarization of light through a prism

Prism In geometry, a prism is a solid object the sides of which are equal *polygons* and the ends equal and parallel polygons. Some prisms are given special names according to the shapes of their bases. Some of the most common shapes are *triangular, quadrangular* and *rhombic*. These names also apply to some crystal structures which grow in the shape of prisms.

Probably the most common use for prisms is in the study of optics. One of the most interesting and simple applications of a triangular glass prism is to the study of the different wave-lengths of light. If the prism is placed in a narrow beam of sunlight, the light will be bent as it passes through the prism. Not all of the colors will be bent in the same amount, however, so that a strip of colors will fall on a screen. This strip of colors is called the SPECTRUM and this method of producing it was discovered by Newton. The violet end of the spectrum is bent through a greater angle than the red end. The separation of the colors by this method is known as *dispersion*.

A rather specialized application of prisms in optics is the *polarization of light*. The prism employed in this process is called a *Nicol prism,* named after its inventor, W. Nicol. The prism is made of two pieces of calcite cut in a particular manner and cemented together with Canada balsam. Because the index of refraction of Canada balsam is between the indices of refraction for the two pieces of the prism, some of the light (extraordinary ray) passes through the prism and the rest of the light (ordinary ray) is reflected out the side. Hence, the light coming out the end is polarized. A. E. L.

SEE ALSO: LENS, MAN-MADE; LIGHT

Privet Privet is a shrub used in hedges. In summer it has small white flowers, and in the fall blue-black berries. Sometimes privet is clipped in odd shapes like arches and animal shapes. It is related to the lilac and the olive.

Probability Probability is a branch of MATHEMATICS that compares the number of ways a particular event may occur to the number of possible outcomes. The probability of choosing a white ball from 3 white and 5 black balls is 3 to 8 or 3/8.

Proboscis (pro-BOS-is) A proboscis is an elongation of the mouth, or an organ which protrudes in the area of the mouth. It may be the sucking organ of an insect or a grasping organ like the elephant's trunk.

Procyon (PROH-see-ahn) Procyon is a brilliant star which gets its name from the fact that it precedes the star *Sirius* in its nightly path across the heavens. Sirius is "the dog" and Procyon means "before the dog."

These two stars are called "dog stars" and are referred to in ancient literature. According to astrology, Procyon is the star that portends wealth, fame, and good luck.

Procyon, like the star SIRIUS, has a faint companion which is believed to be a white dwarf. V. V. N.

Producer Any plant that can make its own food is a producer. All other living things are either *consumers* or *decomposers.*

Producers are eaten by herbivores. Green plants (autotrophs) can take the sun's energy and convert it to chemical energy in the form of carbohydrates, proteins, fats, or vitamins. The ratio of production versus respiration will indicate the energy balance in any given natural community.

Usually a producer makes more food than it requires, and releases excess oxygen. If it did not, all animals would starve to death. Also, plants need the carbon dioxide given off by animals.

The primary producers in the ocean are phytoplanktons; in the prairie, they are the grasses; and in the taiga, the conifers. H.J.C.

Progesterone (pro-JES-ter-own) Certain organic chemicals called *hormones* are necessary for the body to carry on its functions. Progesterone is one of the hormones that regulates the reproductive processes of the female. It circulates in the blood stream.

Progesterone is produced by the *corpus luteum,* a tissue of the OVARY which develops after ovulation. Under the influence of progesterone, the lining of the uterus becomes highly developed and prepared to receive a fertilized egg. The continuous production of progesterone during pregnancy keeps the uterus in the proper condition for the development of the *fetus* or child. J. R. S.

SEE ALSO: ENDOCRINE GLANDS, HORMONE, MENSTRUATION, REPRODUCTIVE SYSTEM

Projectile Any particle or body which has horizontal motion and at the same time acts like a falling body can be classified as a projectile. A stone hurled in a horizontal direction is a projectile. Rifle bullets and torpedoes are the most commonly used examples of projectiles.

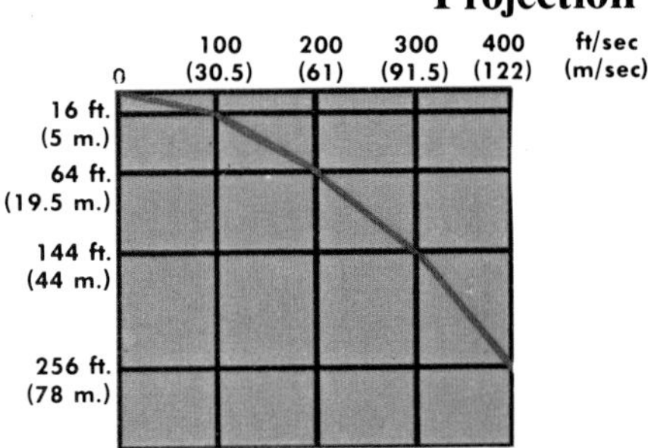

The path of a projectile can be shown on a graph to have a curve as above when the initial velocity is 100 feet (30.5 meters) per second. The fall is due to the regular action of gravity.

If one ignores air resistance, the horizontal motion and vertical motion affect only the path of a projectile and not each other. Hence, the two motions can be studied separately. If a projectile is fired horizontally, it will have a *velocity* in that direction equal to that given it initially. As it is traveling horizontally, it will fall toward earth due to *gravitational* forces exerted on it. While the horizontal motion is at *constant* velocity, the vertical motion is accelerated.

Determining the true paths, called *trajectories,* taken by various projectiles is a very important and complicated mathematical study. For instance, since the trajectory of a rocket is affected by air resistance, air resistance must be taken into account when calculating the trajectory. Further, the trajectory is affected by the speed of the rocket as well as the *rotation of the earth.* The rotation of the earth imparts a horizontal velocity even though the rocket may be fired vertically. Another variable that must be considered is that at some point along the rocket's trajectory, the rocket's speed may enable it to overcome the pull of gravity. A. E. L.

SEE ALSO: MOTION

Projection Projection in MAP-MAKING is the method of representing the surface of the earth, or some other celestial body, on a cylinder, a cone, or an *azimuth.* The best known is the *Mercator* projection in which the earth is presented as a rectangle, with all *parallels* and *meridians* represented by straight lines intersecting at right angles.

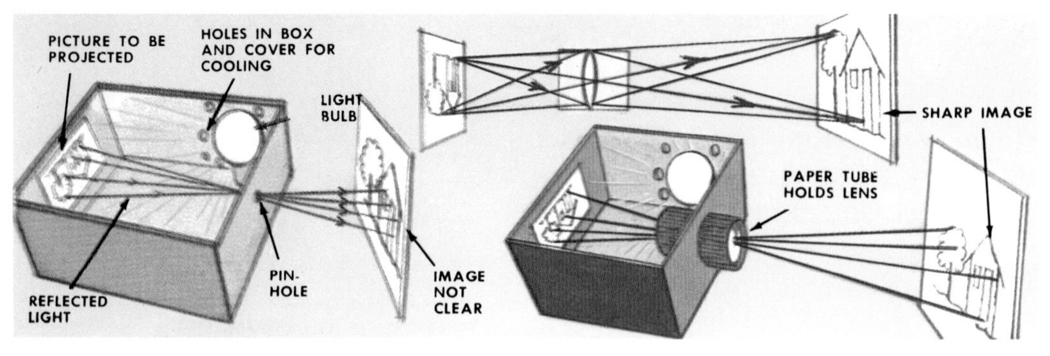

A simple opaque projector; a convex lens fitted to a tube will make a sharper picture

Projector A projector is an optical device which sends out a beam of light. The projector contains a very bright source of light. This light can be gathered and directed by mirrors and lenses. The beam of light can be made to carry an image to be viewed on a screen.

A simple projector throws an image of any small picture onto a table or other surface. A box with ventilation holes on the sides should be big enough to hold a light bulb and the picture to be projected. The light that bounces off the picture will have a path from the box and through the projection hole.

From all parts of the picture, bounced light gets out the hole to strike a screen. An image will show on the screen faintly but rather clearly if the hole is small, and bright but very fuzzy if the hole is large. The viewing screen cannot be very far from the box.

This type is called an *opaque projector*. No light passes through the picture being used. A convex lens fitted into a tube so as to slide and focus at the correct distance from the picture will cast a better image.

A *lantern-slide* type projector requires that light rays pass through a picture. A partly-transparent slide is placed between the light and the projector opening. The image depends on how much light is blocked or colored by the pattern.

How far an image can be projected depends on the brightness of the light source. As light spreads out and covers more screen it becomes more faint. As distance is increased or, for example, doubled (two times as far), the brightness at the screen is one-fourth as much. If ten times as far, the brightness is only one hundredth. Projector bulbs are specially designed so that the filaments concentrate the source of light into a small area. A carbon ARC light is used in movie theatres.

For either opaque or transparent slide projecting, it is important to gather as much light as possible. The more light that bounces off or passes through a picture the brighter the screen image will be. Great amounts of light must pass through a slide film, and it is necessary that the light hitting the film is spread uniformly. White frosted glass is used and called a *diffuser*. Lenses called *condensers* are also used to direct intense beams of light on the film.

The arrangement of lenses that do the final projecting is most important. The bright light that leaves the slide must be brought to a sharp focus. The diagram on the next page uses points of color as they might appear on a cross-section of a slide. It shows they end up on a screen arranged in the same pattern but as a reversed or backward image. Anyone who has threaded a movie projector or slide projector knows that the film piece is fed into the machine upside down and backwards so that it comes out right side up on the screen.

A movie projector rapidly places one picture slide after another between a light

A lantern-slide projector

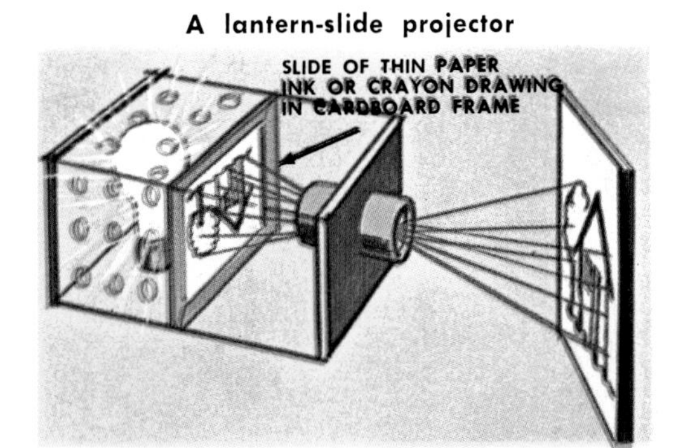

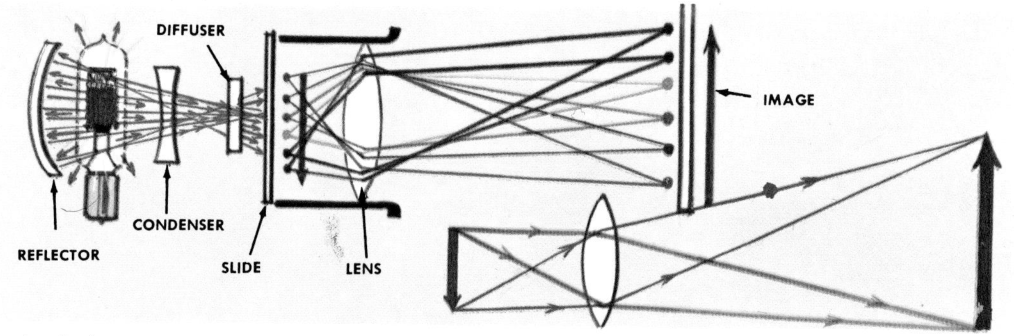

A simple lens system in a projector

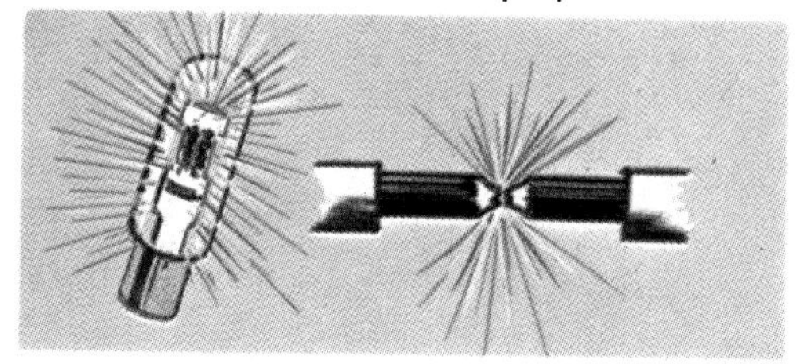
Projector light sources: bulb and carbon arc

source and a system of lenses. A shutter device flashes light just as the pictures come into position, or a special gear jerks the pictures along. A sound movie projector shows twenty-four pictures each second, but the eye sees each flash longer and blends the images together into a moving picture.

The index of refraction for any material varies with the wave-length of light passing through it. Thus, a lens forms an image at a different distance from the lens for each color. The lens in a projector is specially ground to minimize this effect. F. R. W.

SEE ALSO: LENS, MAN-MADE; MOTION PICTURES; PHOTOGRAPHY

Promethium (proh-MEETH-ee-um) Promethium is the rare earth ELEMENT number 61. It does not occur in nature on earth, but does exist in some stars. Promethium is named after Prometheus. According to mythology, Prometheus stole fire from Olympus and gave it to humans.

Promethium was probably first prepared in 1941 at Ohio State University. It was not definitely identified until 1945. A group of scientists at Oak Ridge, Tennessee, consisting of J. Marinsky, C. Coryell, and L. Glendenin, isolated promethium. They used ion-exchange chromotography.

Promethium has 13 known isotopes. Promethium-145 has the longest half-life of 17.7 years. Promethium-147 is used as a fuel for atomic cells. A.J.H.

SEE ALSO: ELEMENTS

Pronghorn see Antelope, Deer family

Prop roots see Banyan, Pandanus

Propagation (prah-puh-GAY-shun) New plants are made from some part of the old plant. A seed will grow into a plant. When a sweet potato is planted in soil it will grow into a plant. A tulip bulb will grow a beautiful flower. A branch of pussy willow when placed in a glass of water will grow new roots. All of these ways that new plants are made are called propagation.

Plants vary as to which part is best for propagating the species. Most annuals are grown from *seed*. In some plants there are many underground stems which are used for propagation instead of the plant's seed. Tulips, daffodils, and onions are *bulbs*. The white potato is a *tuber*, while the sweet potato is a *root*. Iris and quack grass are propagated by *rhizomes*. Crocus and gladiolus have underground stems for propagation called *corms*. The strawberry plant sends a stem along the top of the ground. This runner takes root at certain intervals and starts growing a new plant.

Man has found it more economical and sometimes necessary to use parts of the plant to produce new ones. Banana and seedless fruits must be started from the *root stock* of the mother plant. *Dahlia, manroot,* and *mangel* are produced by *root propagation*. New house plants of *geranium, coleus, ivy,* and *philodendron* can be produced by *cuttings*. A stem from the old plant can be placed in a jar of water until new roots are formed from the cut end of the stem. The LEAVES from *jade, gloxinia,* and *sansevieria* may be placed in moist sand. The end of the *petiole* of the leaf will root and a new plant eventually appears. When cross cuts are made on the veins under a *begonia* leaf and pressed into wet sand, new plants will appear at each cut. Many flowering shrubs can be propagated by cutting a branch off and placing it in a jar of water.

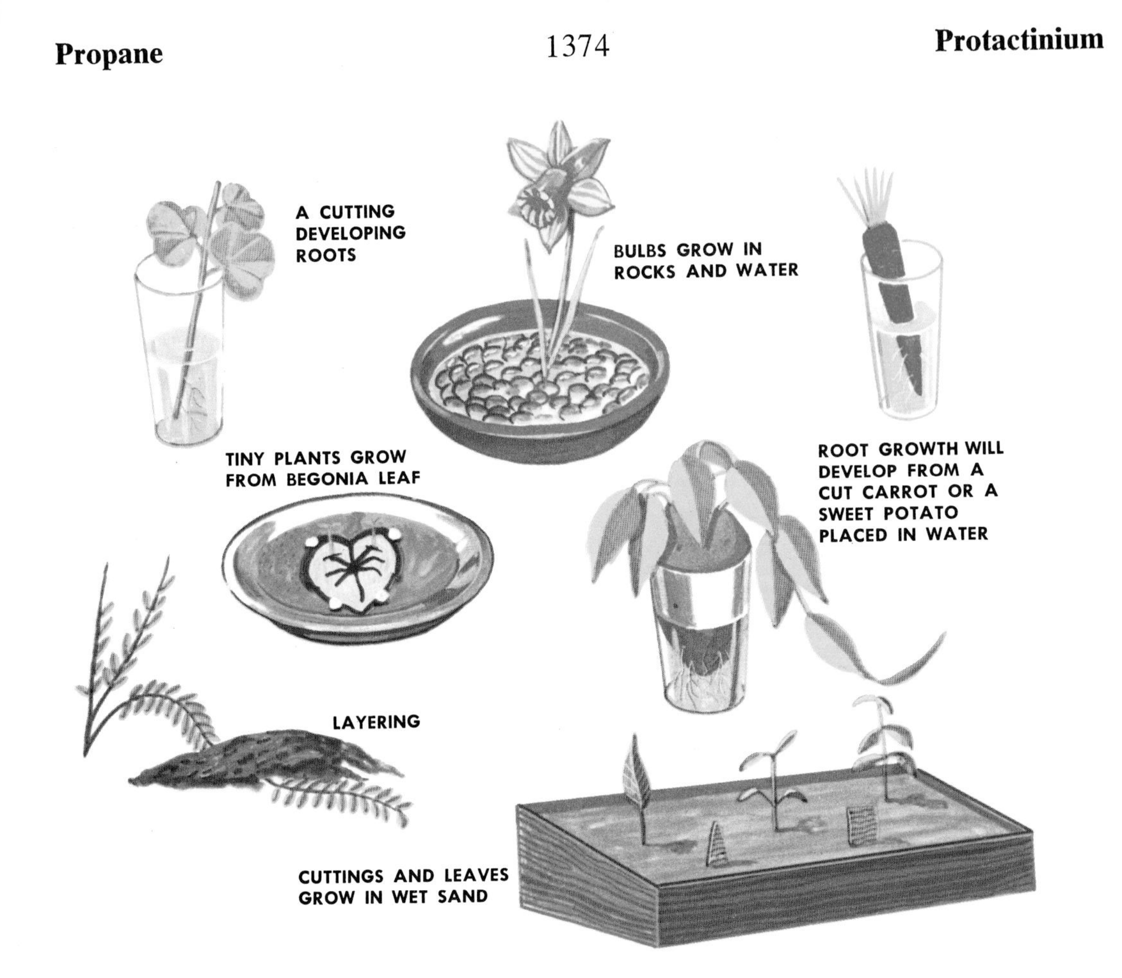

Some home gardeners as well as nurserymen increase their shrub and woody vine supply by a method called *layering.* A branch of the existing plant is pulled over to ground level. At intervals along the branch, soil is piled over it. That part of the branch covered will root and send up a new shoot. When it is well established it can be cut from the original plant.

The propagating medium depends upon the species being produced. *Sand, mica* or *vermiculite,* and *sphagnum moss* are the most successful. Synthetic plant hormones are available. When these are added to the propagating medium they will speed up root growth. H. J. C.

Propane see Methane, Hydrocarbon

Propeller see Aircraft, Airplane

Prophase see Mitosis and meiosis

Proportion Proportion is a statement of equality between two ratios. A RATIO is a relation of one quantity to another. A proportion is written as $a{:}b = c{:}d$ or $\frac{a}{b} = \frac{c}{d}$; a and d are the extremes, and b and c are the means.

Prostate gland see Reproductive systems

Protactinium (proh-tack-TINN-ee-um) Protactinium is a radioactive element whose symbol is Pa. Protactinium has an atomic number of 91 and a mass number of 231. It is found in nature in all uranium ores, and occurs in such ore to the extent of about one-fourth part per million parts of uranium.

An efficient method for separating this element from its ore is a *carrier technique; zirconium phosphate* is precipitated from strong acid solutions, and consequently *precipitates,* or carries down, the solid protactinium with the zirconium salt. Then the protactinium is separated by crystallizing the zirconium as an *oxychloride.* V. V. N.

SEE ALSO: ELEMENTS

Protective coloration Animals have many ways of protecting themselves from their enemies. One way is by being able to fight. Another is by living in places where their enemies cannot get at them. A third way is called *protective coloration*. Animals that have protective coloration are hard to see when they are in the places where they usually live.

Some snakes and insects that live in grass are green. Tropical fish, which are so brightly colored that they are very showy in a tank, can hardly be seen when they are in their natural home among coral and water plants. Some tiny fish are so nearly transparent that they can be seen only when they move.

Even animals whose surroundings change color can sometimes change color to match. Some rabbits and weasels, for instance, shed their brown summer coats and grow white fur in winter. When an animal's body is in shadow, it looks darker than it really is, and many animals, as birds and fish, have undersides that are lighter than their bodies. Since their shadows are underneath them, their lighter bellies look the same color as the rest of them. This type of coloration is called *countershading*.

Another form of protective coloration consists of *patterning*. Stripes and spots make it difficult to see the animal's outline. This is the same principle that man uses in protective camouflage. The dappled back of a baby fawn blends into the leaf-shadows of the woods. Patterning and countershading are important types of protection called *concealing* or *cryptic coloration*.

Mimicry is a form of protective coloration that depends, not on making the animal invisible, but on making it look like something else. A harmless insect may have the same color pattern as one that stings. Shape as well as color may give this kind of protection. The insect known as a WALKING STICK looks like the twig on which it sits. Tree-hoppers are insects that look like thorns. Dead-leaf butterflies are blue and orange when flying, but when they fold their wings, they look like brown leaves.

Not all protective coloration makes the animal inconspicuous. Some animals, such as skunks, are left alone because they are seen and recognized. This is called *warning coloration*. The porcupine has a similar dark and light warning coloration.

Of course, animals cannot voluntarily take on protective coloration. It is one of the characteristics that enable them to survive and have young. Individuals that did not have either protective coloration or some other form of protection have not survived, and so natural selection has favored its development.

M. R. B.

SEE ALSO: BUTTERFLIES, CAMOUFLAGE, EVOLUTION, INSECTA, MIMICRY, MOTH, TROPICAL FISH

✱ THINGS TO DO

WHICH FOODS ARE RICH IN PROTEIN?

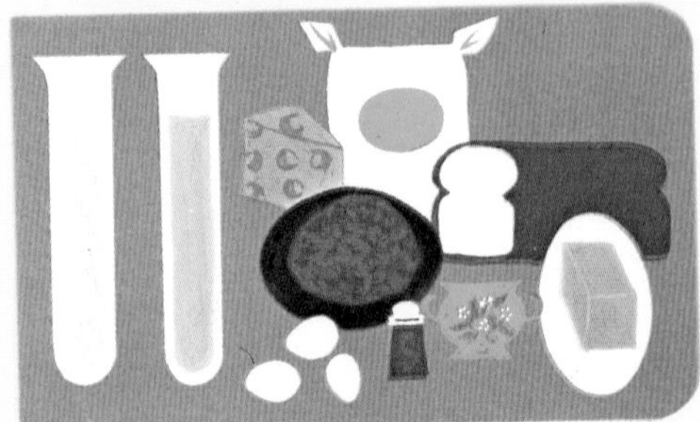

1. **If a food containing protein is mixed with lime and copper sulfate, the mixture will be violet colored.**
2. **Make two solutions and keep them separate until you add a little of each to the food to be tested. Make solution 1 by adding as much copper sulfate as the small amount of water you are using can hold. Make solution 2 by dissolving lime powder in water.**
3. **Add equal parts of these two solutions to the food.**
4. **Is there protein in the following foods: hamburger, flour, butter, eggs, sugar, salt, cheese, and bread? Do some of these appear to have more protein than others?**

Protein All living things are made up of cells. These cells are made up of protoplasm which is largely a mixture of proteins. The Greek word *proteios* from which protein is derived means "primary." These materials are of first or primary importance in living things.

Most proteins are very large molecules containing hundreds of atoms of CARBON, HYDROGEN, OXYGEN, NITROGEN, and often SULFUR.

During the digestive process, proteins are broken into *amino acids* by the addition of water molecules (*hydrolysis*). Adult intestinal cells are usually unable to absorb protein molecules, but they can absorb amino acids.

There are 22 amino acids important to living cells. All amino acid molecules have an NH_2, or amino, group. The molecules end with the organic acid, or *carboxyl*, group (COOH).

Amino acids are sent from the digestive tract to the LIVER. From there, they might either be sent into the blood to be used by cells to build new structures, or, the amino group might be chemically removed from the amino acid molecule. The amino group would then be made into UREA and sent to the kidneys for excretion as part of the urine. The rest of the amino acid molecule would then be changed to sugar.

Fourteen of the amino acids can be made in the body. Eight of them cannot; either the proper "raw materials" (*metabolites*) or the correct ENZYMES for making them are lacking in cells. These eight must be obtained from protein foods. J. C. K.

SEE ALSO: AMINO ACIDS, CARBOHYDRATES, NUTRITION, STARCHES, NUCLEOPROTEIN

Proterozoic Era (proh-ter-uh-ZOH-ick) The Proterozoic Era (*proto* means "earlier" and *zoic* means "life") occurred from 1,700 million years ago to 600 million years ago. It lasted 1,200 million years.

The Proterozoic Era was part, along with the ARCHEOZOIC ERA, of the *Pre-Cambrian* period. Pre-Cambrian rocks of these eras include *igneous, sedimentary,* and *metamorphic* rocks. Signs of past life are most often found in the sedimentary rocks. Even in these rocks very few distinct proterozoic fossils have been found. The lime deposits of blue-green ALGAE are the only known plant fossils. Animal fossils are even more rare and less distinct. They include the marine worms, jellyfish, sponges, and one-celled protozoans.

These plants and animals were all marine forms. Apparently no life existed on land. Because remains of very simple marine life occur in the rocks of this time, one can conclude that there probably was a good deal of such life in the oceans. The lack of fossils can be explained by the fact that most forms were very small and lacked hard parts such as shells, bones, etc., that could be preserved as fossils.

During this part of the Pre-Cambrian period intensive *volcanism* and *diastrophism* (uplifting) occurred. It was, however, interrupted by long periods of *erosion* and *deposition.* There was also another very important event. The first recorded *Ice Age* of the earth's history took place in eastern

Fossil remains of Pre-Cambrian worms

Canada. Geologists know this because it left *striated* boulders and other glacial deposits as evidence of its occurrence.

These mountain-building revolutions were not sudden, short periods of upheavals, but are known to have been many millions of years in length. V. V. N.

SEE ALSO: GEOLOGIC TIME TABLE

Proton (elementary particle) (PRO-tahn) Protons are matter that has never been seen. Each proton has a positive *electric* charge, infinite life, and a mass of 1.67 x 10^{27} kg. Protons exist in all atomic nuclei. They are about 398 trillion times as dense as water molecules. In 1919, RUTHERFORD suggested the name "proton." Recent research has shown that the proton itself is surrounded by a "cloud" of MESONS.

The mass of a proton is 1.00759 atomic mass units (amu). The modern standard of atomic weight, adopted in 1960, assigns the carbon 12 ISOTOPE a mass of exactly 12 units.

High energy protons are produced in accelerators, such as cyclotrons. When the nuclei of other atoms are bombarded by protons, new elements are formed. These elements are often radioactive. Very high energy protons have great penetrating power. A proton having an energy of 450 million electron volts can penetrate more than 3 feet (.9 meter) of water. The proton gradually loses energy as it passes through the water. The average distance a proton travels before all its energy is lost is called the *range* of the proton.

Low energy protons in the form of hydrogen ions, H^+, are responsible for the acidic properties of substances such as hydrochloric acid (HCl), sulfuric acid (H_2SO_4), and acetic acid ($HC_2H_3O_2$). J. H. D.

SEE ALSO: ATOM, NUCLEAR SCIENCE

Proton number see Atomic number in Nuclear glossary

✳ THINGS TO DO

HOW MANY ANIMALS CAN YOU FIND IN A DROP OF WATER?

1 One-celled animals are found in most fresh water, streams, ponds, lakes, or classroom aquariums.

2 Take a large jar along with you when collecting. Fill the jar with an inch of mud from the bottom of the pond and then half full of pond water. Break off a handful of dried hay or grass growing along the bank. Add this to your culture.

3 Cook up about a dozen grains of rice. This will serve as additional food. Permit the jar to stand for one week undisturbed. Do not put it in direct sunlight.

4 Put a drop of this protozoa culture on a slide and observe under a microscope. It will be teeming with one-celled animals, as well as minute water insects, and flatworms.

Protoplasm Protoplasm is the general name for the living material of which all plant and animal CELLS are made. In cells, protoplasm is divided into a usually centrally placed *nucleus* and its surrounding *cytoplasm*.

Protozoa (proh-tuh-ZOH-uh) *Protozoa* means "first animal." Many scientists think that *Protozoa,* or animals like them, were the first animals to live on the earth. They are classed as the first, or simplest, group of lower animals because their bodies are made of a single cell. They are called *unicellular* animals. *Uni* means "one."

People are made up of many tiny cells, which cannot be seen with the naked eye. For the same reason, most people have never seen protozoa. If five of the largest were placed end to end, they would take up only 1 inch (2.5 centimeters). It would take 25,000 of the smallest to measure 1 inch (2.5 centimeters).

Even though each protozoan animal has only one cell, it takes in food, water, and oxygen. Protozoa build new materials for their cells and get rid of wastes. Like the larger animals with many cells, the protozoa are able to carry on all the activities that are necessary to stay alive.

All protozoa live in water. They may, however, live in microscopic bits of water. Those which live in the dry desert sand need only the thin film of water found between particles of sand. These small creatures have neither limbs nor muscles to travel great distances. Nevertheless, they are carried all over the world by wind, water, and other animals.

MOVEMENT OF PROTOZOA

According to the way they move from place to place, the protozoa have been divided into five large groups or classes. The *Flagellata,* or "whip-bearers," have one or more long flagella by which they swim. The flagella is a thin thread-like extension of the protoplasm, located at the front end of the body. As it is vibrated in a whip-like motion, the animal is towed behind.

The *ameboid* protozoa are called the *Sarcodina* after the Greek word *sarcos,* meaning "flesh." These animals put out *pseudopods,* or false feet, which are only temporary extensions of the protoplasm. Thus their bodies are continually changing shape. Since some members, like the *radiolarians,* are covered with shells, they must push the protoplasm through tiny holes in the shell.

The *Ciliata* are a group of agile protozoa which move by means of *cilia,* short hair-

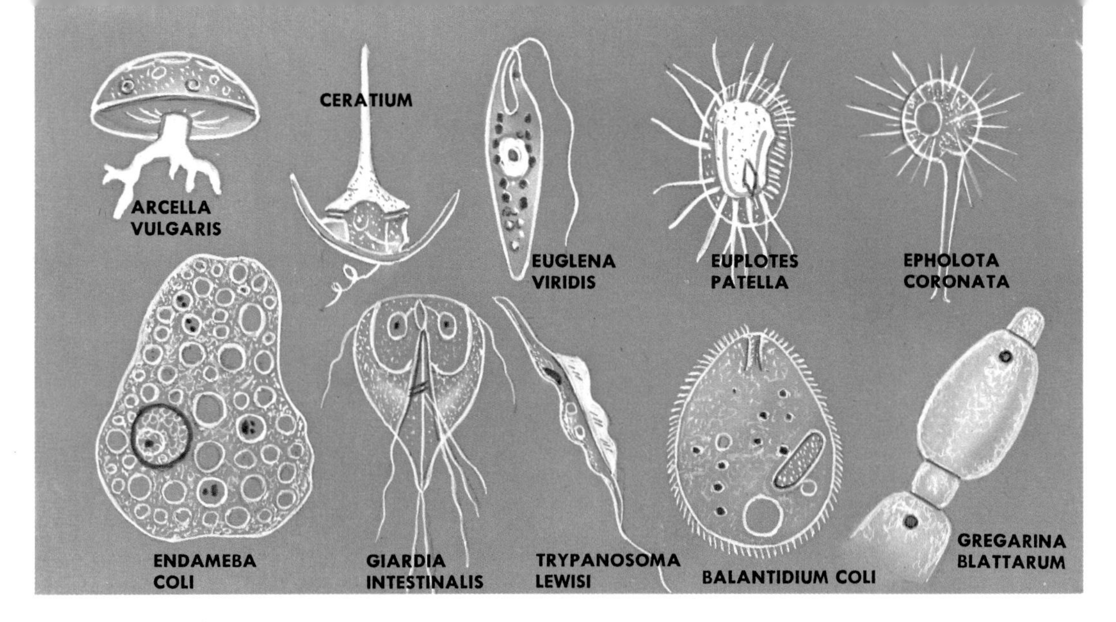

Various protozoa with scientific names; top row are free-living, bottom are parasitic

like extensions of the protoplasm. By beating these rows of cilia, the animal is propelled much as a boat is rowed with oars.

Some members of the *Sporozoa* are enemies of man, since they cause such diseases as malaria and cattle fever. These protozoa have no particular type of locomotion because they are all parasitic. Instead, they rely upon water and animals to transport their spores, or offspring.

The *Suctoria,* or sucking protozoa, make up a special class. Although the young move by means of cilia, the adults attach themselves permanently to a solid surface. Since they have a long stalk and sucking *tentacles,* they resemble a tiny plant.

HOW THEY EAT

The method of obtaining food ranges from plant-like to animal-like habits. Some of the flagellates are able to carry on photosynthesis like a green plant, since their bodies contain chlorophyll. They manufacture and store starch from the food in water and soil. Other protozoa, like the large carnivorous animals, chase their prey. Some feed upon both plants and animals. BACTERIA, ALGAE, wood particles, and other small animals are common foods.

Some protozoa, like *Paramecium,* have permanent mouths or surfaces for ingesting food. The ameboid protozoa, however, take in food at any point on their bodies. The protoplasm simply flows around the piece of food. Suctorians have a unique method of sucking up the protoplasm of their prey by means of their long tentacles. Most parasites and many flagellates have another method. They absorb foods which have already been broken down into simpler substances.

THE PARTS OF THE BODY

Although each species is different in structure, all protozoa consist of a mass of living protoplasm which is surrounded by a thin membrane. For protection, there is often a thick, outer cuticle. Some have beautiful calcium or glassy shells.

Perhaps the most conspicuous parts of the cell are the *nucleus, food vacuole,* and *contractile vacuoles.* The nucleus is the controller of the cell, regulating all chemical processes. From two to many hundreds of nuclei may be present. Food vacuoles, present only after eating, are large droplets of water containing food. Instead of food vacuoles, protozoa which photosynthesize food have pigment bodies containing chlorophyll. For collecting excess fluid from the protoplasm, one or more contractile vacuoles are present.

SELF-PRESERVATION

To protect themselves, to rest, or to reproduce, many protozoa surround their bodies with a thick-walled sac, or cyst. This is practiced among most parasitic protozoa, especially as they move from host to host. When environmental conditions are unfavorable in deserts, ponds, and marshes, this covering becomes necessary for survival.

While reproduction is sometimes sexual, most protozoa produce new animals by *asexual* means. Some develop buds which break off, while others divide one or more times in order to produce two or more daughter cells. E. P. L.

SEE ALSO: AMEBA; ANIMALS, CLASSIFICATION OF; CELLS; EUGLENA; EVOLUTION; MALARIA; PARAMECIUM; PARASITES; REPRODUCTION, ASEXUAL; STENTOR; VOLVOX

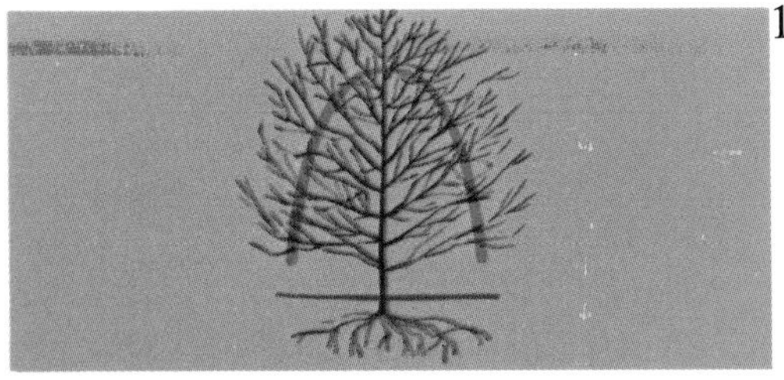

Shrub branches are pruned to increase bloom

Pruning This is a process of cutting back certain parts of a plant. It is done naturally by strong winds, heavy ice or snow on branches, too much fruit, or lack of sun. Pruning is also done by man.

Man prunes trees and shrubs with sharp instruments. Antiseptics applied to large wounds prevent infections. Pruning gives a plant a better shape, increases the size of flowers, improves fruit production, and lengthens plant life. It also removes diseased parts.

Spring-blooming shrubs and trees should be pruned after the flowers fall. Late bloomers should be pruned in the winter or very early spring. The time of year best for pruning depends on the various species. H. J. C.

Prune (fruit) see Plum

Pseudopodia Pseudopodia are temporary extensions of the body of a one-celled animal such as the ameba. They make possible a flowing type of movement or engulfing of food.

SEE: AMEBA, PROTOZOA

Psychedelic (sye-ka-DELL-ic) This means *mind-changing* and refers to a group of drugs that produce *hallucinations*. Some of these drugs occur naturally in plants; others can be produced by combining chemicals.

People have used psychedelic drugs for centuries. The Vikings chewed poisonous mushrooms before battle to gather courage or to drive themselves *berserk*. Aztec Indians used poisonous mushrooms in religious ceremonies. Indian members of the Native American Church drink tea made from the *peyotyl* cactus or chew parts of the plant, producing hallucinations.

LSD-25 (lysergic acid diethylamide) is one of a number of synthetic hallucinogens. A more powerful chemical is STP. Depending on the drug, hallucinogens are either taken by mouth, sniffed through the nose, or injected. Different people react differently to different hallucinogenic drugs. Generally, however, the overall effect is a distorted reality. Colors may become vivid and flowing. A person may feel lost from his body. Some people have been killed in impossible attempts while on hallucinogens. The length of time a drug affects a person's perceptions varies widely, ranging all the way from one or two hours to several days.

These drugs appear to have some beneficial medical uses. They can be helpful in cases of alcoholism and nervous disorders. Indiscriminate use, however, may lead to severe anxiety, panic, psychosis, or suicide. Although these drugs are not known to be physically addicting, a person may become psychologically dependent on them. B. M. H.

SEE ALSO: ADDICTION, DRUGS, NARCOTICS, SCHIZOPHRENIA

Psychology (sye-KAHL-uh-jee) Psychology is a behavioral science that studies and tries to explain behavior of both humans and animals. The word is from two Greek roots, *psyche* meaning "mind" and *logos* meaning "study of". The many different fields of psychology fall into two basic categories: *research,* which tries to develop theories that explain certain behaviors; and *applied,* which uses those theories to solve problems.

The differences between research and applied psychology are often fuzzy. Research psychologists perform tests to develop theories; applied psychologists use these theories in solving problems. For example, a research psychologist might state that people are more productive in their work if their jobs are less structured. An industrial psychologist might use this theory to solve a production problem in a factory. This psychologist might change the way the work is done. The psychologist might put workers in teams, and let each team be responsible for building an entire product—for example, an automobile—

San Diego Zoo

Psychologists deal extensively with laboratory animals in developing their theories. Chimpanzees, with their high intelligence, have been taught sign language, and some can communicate simple thoughts to their testers.

rather than having individuals just do one type of job all day. Theory is then tested in actual working conditions, and the problem is solved if the theory is correct.

FIELDS OF PSYCHOLOGY

Psychology is wide-ranging in scope, and includes many areas of study. In the research category, some areas include experimental, learning, physiological, and social psychology.

Experimental psychologists develop theories from carefully controlled experiments, usually performed in a laboratory setting. They might experiment with rats running mazes to see if the amount of sleep that the rats get affects their performance in the maze; they might use people in a group situation to see what kind of help or comfort adults will give a crying child; or any other situation where the circumstances are controlled. They also study control groups, where they observe "normal" behavior, as when the stimulus of the crying child is removed.

Learning psychologists investigate how and why living things learn a behavior and remember that behavior. They might attempt to explain why one child can't read well while another child from the same family reads very well. Learning psychology is often applied to school situations to help all students learn basic skills well.

Physiological psychology tries to relate behavior to body processes. This might include studies of hormones and how they affect moods and behaviors of people, or perhaps the effect of vitamin deficiencies on the behavior of children.

Social psychology tries to explain behavior between groups and the influence that groups have in shaping individuals' behaviors. Some areas that are explored in this field are prejudice, conformity, and conflicts within a group.

Some applied psychology fields include educational, counseling, industrial, and the largest sub-field of psychology, clinical psychology.

Educational psychologists attempt to use learning theories to develop new methods of teaching. *Counseling* psychologists work with individuals who may be trying to make career or education choices, with families that are having difficulties in solving conflicts, or with people who are faced with difficult decisions. *Industrial* psychologists help individuals adjust to the demands of their jobs and work with employers to create a good system and atmosphere in which to work.

Clinical psychology is the largest of the specialized fields. These psychologists work with people who are emotionally disturbed, often as part of a team with a psychiatrist and a social worker. They may work in clinics or hospitals. They often research a patient's background and help in diagnosing and treating the patient. They are trained in therapy techniques, and may work either on an individual or a group basis. They try to help patients deal more effectively with the circumstances of their life and their environment.

Psychology is often confused with *psychiatry*. Psychiatry is a medical field that uses various treatments, such as drugs and shock therapy, in addition to therapy techniques, to treat mentally ill patients. Psychology is a broader field. It includes the study of all behavior, both normal and abnormal. Psychologists also use therapy techniques in treating disturbed patients, but that is only one area of specialization in this broad field. Ed.

SEE ALSO: NERVOUS SYSTEM; PAVLOV, IVAN; REFLEX; SCIENTIFIC METHOD; STATISTICS; STIMULUS

Psyllium

Psyllium (SIL-ee-uhm) Psyllium seed is often used in medicine. It comes from a European species of plantain (*Plantago psyllium*). Most plantains are common weeds.

Ptarmigan see Grouse

Pterodactyl (ter-uh-DACK-tihl) The pterodactyl was a flying reptile that lived more than 60 million years ago. Although it could fly, it was not a bird. It had certain features similar to birds, but basically it was a reptile.

The pterodactyl belonged to a group of reptiles which lived during the MESOZOIC ERA when the great reptiles roamed the earth. The flying reptiles are referred to as *pterosaurs,* a word made from the Greek word *pteron* meaning "wing" and *sauros,* "lizard." These pterosaurs had forelimbs or arm-like parts adapted for flying or gliding instead of walking. Their bones were hollow as are the similar bones of birds today. They had no feathers, however. The wings were formed of a leathery membrane extending from a foreleg finger to the body, probably similar to that of the modern bat. The pterodactyl's hind legs were long and slender; its tail was generally short.

Pterodactyls ranged from those with 1-foot (.3-meter) wingspreads to the *Pteranodon,* with a 20-foot (6.1-meter) wingspread. It had a long skull, no teeth, and a short tail. All forms are extinct today.

SEE ALSO: BIRD, DINOSAUR, REPTILIA D.J.I.

Pteranodon, the largest of the pterodactyls

Chicago Natural History Museum

Ptolemy (TAHL-uh-mee) (127-151) Ptolemy (Claudius Ptolemaeus) was a noted Greek astronomer, geographer, and mathematician who lived in the second century A.D. He is best known for his system of astronomy, the *Ptolemaic System,* which declared the earth to be the center of the universe. His theory of the universe was believed by most people to be true until NICOLAUS COPERNICUS, a Polish monk, proved in the sixteenth century that the sun, and not the earth, is the center of the solar system.

Almost nothing is known about the life of Ptolemy. It is generally believed that he was born at Ptolemaius Hermii, a Grecian city in Egypt. The period of his life is estimated from the dates of his astronomical observations. It is believed that he made his observations and wrote in Alexandria.

The most important of Ptolemy's works was the *Almagest,* a thirteen-volume abstract of the astronomical science of the Alexandrian Greeks. In it Ptolemy explained his system of astronomy, giving Hipparchus credit as his chief authority. The system Ptolemy advanced was one in which the earth was a motionless globe. Around it revolved a spherical transparent shell in which were located forty-eight constellations and seven planets: the Moon, Mercury, Venus, the Sun, Mars, Jupiter, and Saturn. While making his observations, he discovered the irregular motion of the moon in orbit called *evection.*

Although Ptolemy is thought to have studied mathematics to make his astronomical observations more meaningful, his mathematical discoveries proved to be of greater value than those in astronomy. By explaining the mathematical theories of Hipparchus, he is considered by some to be the founder of *plane* and *spherical trigonometry.*

As a geographer, Ptolemy was almost entirely in error. He did, however, summarize all that the ancient world knew about the surface features of the earth. His main contribution to geography was an eight-volume *Guide to Geography,* the earliest effort to treat geography scientifically. He did not mention climate, natural resources, people, or unique physical features of the countries with which he dealt. His map of the world and his twenty-six colored maps showed knowledge quite in advance of his time. The *Guide* greatly influenced the future study of geography. D. H. J.

SEE ALSO: ASTRONOMY, SOLAR SYSTEM

Ptomaine (TOH-mayn) Ptomaine is a word derived from the Greek word *ptoma* meaning "corpse." It is a term applied to substances (organic bases) which are formed by the action of bacteria on animal or plant matter, causing decay.

It is a compound containing nitrogen, produced by the putrefaction of proteins. Most ptomaines are harmless, but a few may be poisonous.

For a long time it was believed that the intestinal disturbance known as ptomaine poisoning was caused by eating food containing ptomaines. It has been established by medical authorities that this is not so, but that food poisoning is caused by specific bacterial poisons in spoiled food. W. J. K.

Puberty (PYOO-ber-tee) Puberty, or *adolescence,* is the time in a person's life when he or she begins to look more like an adult than a child. This happens anywhere between the ages of 10 and 14. It is the beginning of social and sexual maturity.

In both males and females, puberty is marked by the development of hair in the armpits and the pubic regions. Sweat glands begin producing more sweat. Hormone levels rise, and both sexes find themselves growing taller because of a growth hormone. (Females sometimes experience this spurt in height before males of the same age.)

For a male, puberty involves the growth of hair on the face, deepening of the voice, growth of the sex organs, and, through hormone change, the ability to produce SPERM. His muscles become more developed, and his shoulders and chest become wider.

Puberty in a female means the gradual growth of breasts and the widening of the hips. She begins to *menstruate.* After MENSTRUATION begins she starts to produce

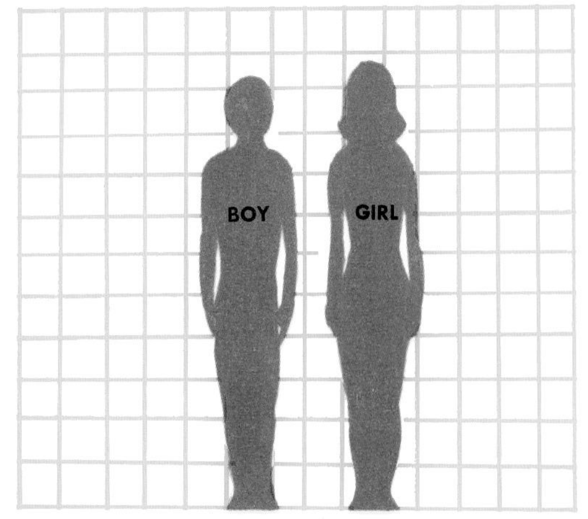

At twelve years, the girl is larger and more mature than the boy

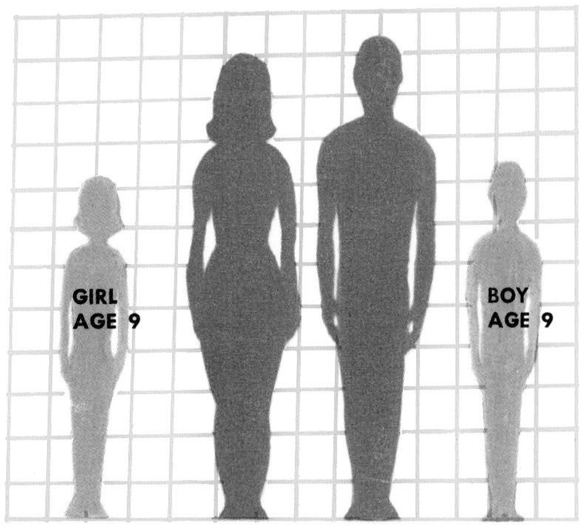

At fifteen the boy is usually larger and heavier than the girl. Adult body characteristics have begun to appear

OVA (eggs) from her ovaries.

Puberty is a gradual process. Often young people going through puberty worry because other people of their own age are maturing faster than they are. But each person matures at his or her own pace. Besides physical changes, a person going through puberty may become confused by the changes in his or her body, and may have a hard time understanding new feelings about himself or herself. He or she may start to question the world around him or her, and to become more independent. When a person becomes confused, sometimes it is helpful to discuss feelings with an understanding older person. Ed.

SEE ALSO: HORMONES, PITUITARY, REPRODUCTIVE SYSTEMS, SEX

Puff adder see Snakes

Puffin

Puffin Puffin is a seabird of the AUK family. It has black-and-white plumage, a ducklike body, and short legs which make walking difficult. It is noted for its large, brightly-colored, triangular beak.

SEE: BIRD

Pulley see Machines, simple

Pulsars Pulsars (pulsating radio stars) were discovered in 1967 by Anthony Hewish. He identified them as rotating *neutron stars.*

Neutron stars have roughly the mass of our sun, compressed into a ball about 5 miles (8 kilometers) in diameter. When they rotate, pulsars emit X-ray bursts, sometimes every few seconds (the first studied emitted pulses at the rate of one every 1.33730113 seconds). Some pulse rates slow down, while others speed up, or "glitch." Astronomers attribute glitches to starquakes, in which a neutron star readjusts its shape. A.J.D./D.D.

SEE ALSO: QUASARS, STARS

Pulse The pulse is a rhythmic beat felt in any artery close to the skin. The contraction of the heart forces blood into the arteries, the arteries expand, and this expansion can be felt as beating or throbbing.

SEE: ARTERY, BLOOD, BLOOD PRESSURE, CIRCULATORY SYSTEM

Puma see Cat family

Pumice Pumice is formed as steam and other gases bubble through LAVA. It is a very lightweight, porous rock, has a spongy appearance, and will float on water. It is used as an abrasive, usually in powdered form.

SEE ALSO: ROCKS

Pump A pump is a machine made to raise or move liquids or gases by suction or pressure.

Pumps serve many purposes. In rural areas, hand or electric-powered pumps lift water from a well. A pump removes water from washing machines. Pumps circulate water, gasoline, and oil within an automobile engine. Large electric pumps force water to houses in the city. Oil, gasoline, and natural gas are transported hundreds of miles through pipe lines by means of pumps. The animal heart is a very important pump.

One of the earliest known pumps was the Egyptian "chain of pots." This pump obtained water from the Nile river. Romans used pumps in connection with their skillfully-developed aqueduct and city water system.

Today, many types of pumps perform various jobs. Basically, pumps fall into three classifications: (1) *suction* or *reciprocating* pumps, including lift pumps, (2) *force* pumps, and (3) *centrifugal* pumps.

The suction pump is often found on farms. It consists of a piston which fits air-tight into a barrel or tube. On the piston, a valve opens upward. A handle is attached to a rod; and, in turn, the rod moves the piston up and down. At the bottom of the tube is another valve which also opens upward. When the handle moves the piston downward, the air in the tube is pushed out through the valve on the piston. When the piston is moved upward, gravity closes this valve and produces a partial VACUUM above the water in the bottom of the tube. The water is forced upward into the tube by the pressure of the air on the surface of the water in the well. After a few strokes of the handle, the tube is filled and water flows out the spout. Since it depends on air pressure, it can lift water only to a height equal to that pressure, about 32 feet (9.7 meters).

A lift pump is a variety of the common suction pump. This type of pump is placed at the bottom of a well. It relies less upon the efficiency of its suction, but relies more on mechanically lifting water.

The force pump has no valve in the piston,

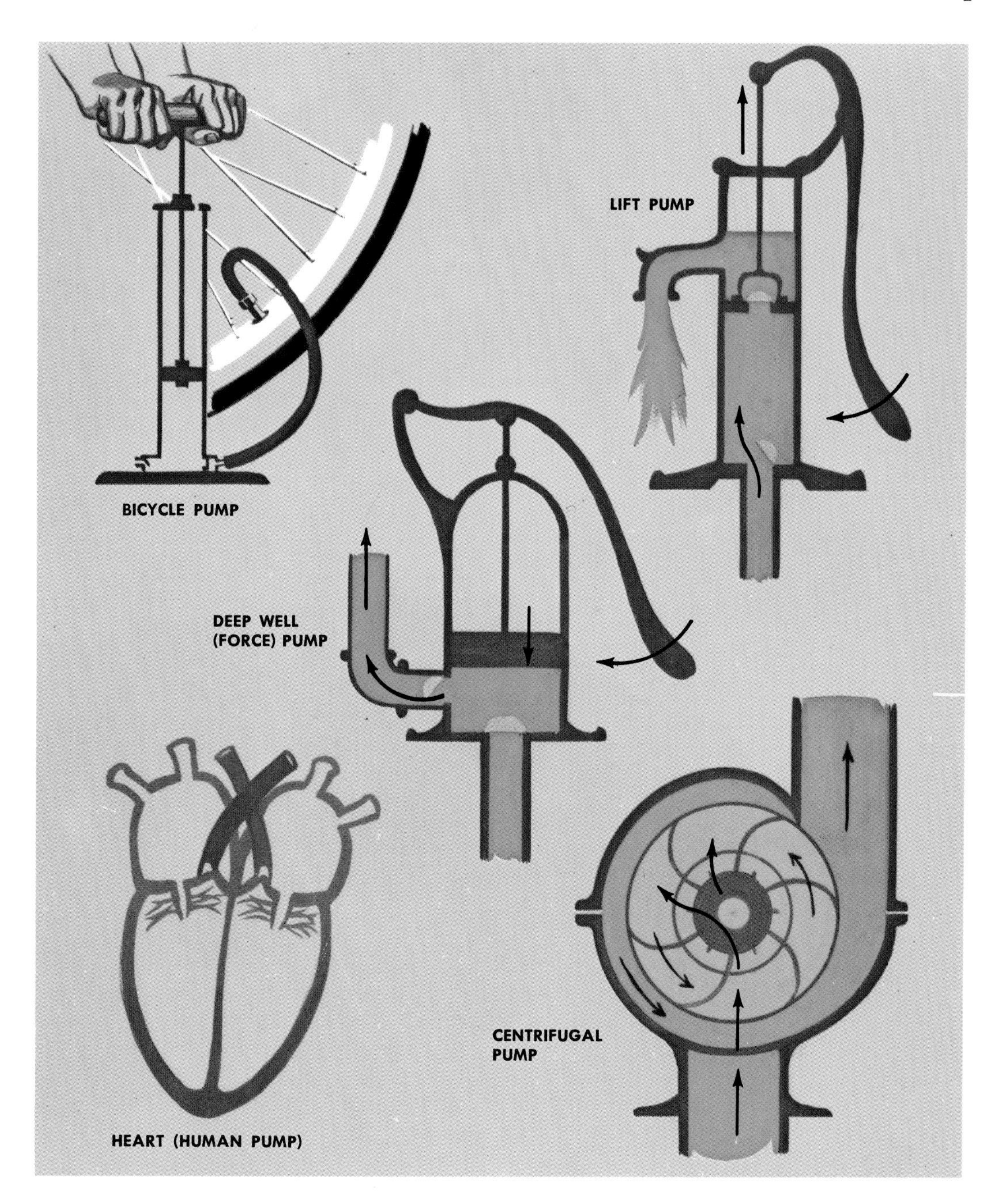

but rather has a valve at the spout or delivery tube. This type of pump is used in deep wells and by fire engines. It works independently of air pressure. Force pumps are usually run by electric or gasoline engines.

A *mercury vapor* pump uses mercury as a piston. By removing mercury from a bulb or tube, a vacuum is created. Early light bulbs had air removed from them by this type of pump.

Centrifugal pumps are employed for removing a large quantity of water or other liquid, provided the lift is not great. Generally, a centrifugal pump consists of a fan-shaped *impeller,* or blade. Inlets lead from the pump's center to its outer edge. An outlet is located on the edge of the pump. The impeller rotates rapidly, thus pumping the water by centrifugal force to the outlet. Washing machines use centrifugal pumps to pump out water. Modern water and sewage plants use this type of pump. P. F. D.

SEE ALSO: WELL

Pumpkin and vine

Pumpkin The fruit of the annual pumpkin plant is large and fleshy. The leaves are broad and lobed. The climbing stem develops tendrils that curl around things.

Insects carry the pollen from the male flower to the female flower. The resulting edible berry-like fruit is often called a *pepo*.

Pumpkin seeds may be fried and salted for eating, and the field pumpkin is used for cattle feed. The pie pumpkin is usually made from *Cucurbita maxima,* a squash plant. Both pumpkin and squash are in the gourd family. H. J. C.

Pupa see Metamorphosis

Pupil see Eye

Pure culture see Bacteriology

Purification Over the years, drinking water has been the most serious source of epidemic diseases. Many of the illnesses were traced directly to water that was not pure. Fortunately, the public water supplies today, particularly in the communities of this country, are well cared for. One rarely even gives thought to the safety of the water he uses.

Although purification is expensive, everyone should realize how important it is to protect and safeguard the water supplies. Whenever a community becomes careless about water, the threat of an epidemic of typhoid fever or other diseases may become serious.

Water supplies can be divided into two general groups: surface and underground. Surface-water supplies come from streams and lakes. Water from these sources is not considered safe unless it has been purified. Underground water supplies are obtained

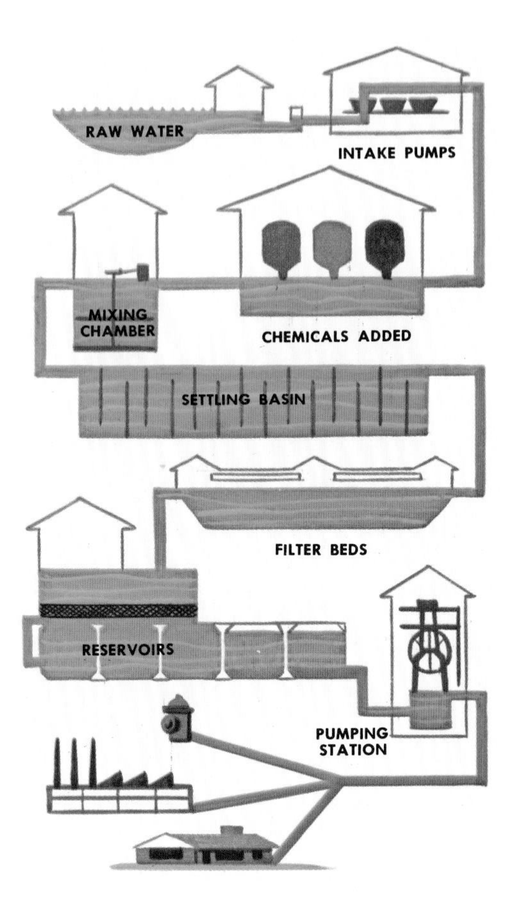

from springs and drilled wells. This water is usually safe provided it has not been contaminated with surface water or by drainage. This type of water supply should be tested periodically.

The water supplies of large communities are usually from lakes and streams, and therefore, it must go through a purification process. Two factors should be considered to make water fit for human consumption. First, the dissolved organic matter should be removed. Second, the bacteria must be destroyed. Almost all towns and cities use one or more of the following methods.

Settling: Water flows slowly into tanks, reservoirs, or basins. It is here that the organic matter sinks slowly to the bottom. Then the water is allowed to flow off on the opposite side of the settling basin from which it entered.

Chemicals: Particles of organic matter will settle more rapidly if certain chemicals such as alum are added to the settling tanks.

Filtration: Water is allowed to settle slowly through layers of sand, gravel, or

✳ THINGS TO DO

SETTING UP A FILTERING PLANT

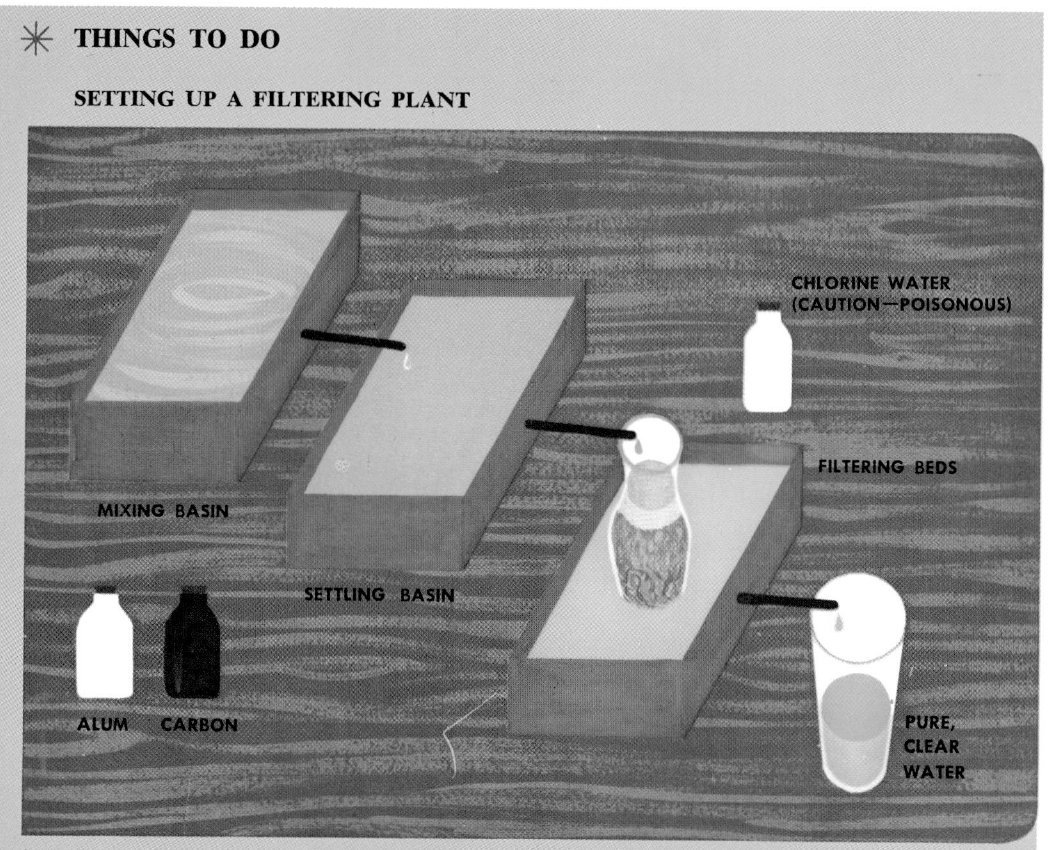

1 Raw lake or river water must be treated before it is safe to drink. A model waterworks plant may be assembled by following the illustration.

2 Metal pans may be used for the mixing and settling basins. A glass chimney is suitable for the filtering bed. You will need to purchase alum which helps to clump the foreign particles and algae in the water to hasten the settling action. Carbon removes the fishy odors often found in water. Put a piece of gauze over the lower opening of the chimney. Add a layer of small pebbles on the bottom, then a layer of coarse sand, and finally fine sand. In water plants, a small amount of chlorine (poisonous) is added to kill the bacteria.

3 The final product should be clean clear water safe for drinking but since your model is on such a small scale it probably will not do a very efficient job.

charcoal. It loses much of its organic matter in this way and leaves as clear water

Aeration: In many reservoirs, fountains force water up into the air. Here oxygen is dissolved in water and the flat taste is improved. Germs that are present are killed by the sunlight.

Chlorination: The gas chlorine is one of the most effective chemicals used to kill bacteria. It is used extensively in water purification. Many cities add this chemical to their water supply regularly, while others do so only when the bacteria count is higher than safety allows.

Fluoridation: Many cities now add fluoride salts to their water. Fluoride in low concentrations can be a means of reducing the occurence of cavities in children's teeth. There is also some evidence that dental cavities are decreased in adults.

Desalination: The shortage of fresh water has prompted a considerable amount of research on the purification of salt water. In the reverse osmosis process, salt water under pressure is brought into contact with a semi-permeable membrane. The water passes through the membrane leaving the salt behind. Other methods are also being developed. V.V.N.

SEE ALSO: ENGINEERING, WATER

Pussy willows with catkins

Purine (PYOOR-een) Purine is an organic compound, containing atoms of carbon and nitrogen. The atoms are arranged to form a double ring. One ring is six-sided and the other has five sides. Purine rings give rise to such compounds as caffeine in coffee beans and tea leaves.

Adenine and guanine are derived from purine. These compounds are part of the nucleoproteins important to heredity. When a cell breaks down adenine and guanine, a substance called uric acid is formed. Uric acid is excreted by the kidneys as a part of urine.

A cell can make new adenine and guanine from the amino acid glycine. Cells may obtain glycine from digested protein foods (milk, eggs, meat) or "make" it from other amino acids. J. C. K.

SEE ALSO: NUCLEOPROTEINS, PROTEIN

Pus Pus is a semi-solid, yellowish discharge which appears at the site of an INFECTION. It is composed of dead *leucocytes, lymph, microorganisms,* and other debris.

Pussy willow The pussy willow is a shrub in the willow family (*Salicaceae*). When the early spring flower buds open, the young male flowers are furry and soft. They look like small gray kittens clinging to the branches. Later the flowers become long graceful catkins.

Leaves appear after the pussy willow flowers. They are smooth and long, bright green above and gray underneath. The catkins develop into larger clusters and are covered with yellow pollen and then form seeds or drop off the bush.

Pussy willows grow wild in low, wet spots, sometimes reaching 25 feet (7.6 meters). They are planted to beautify a place and to attract songbirds. P.G.B.

Putty Putty is a fine powdered CHALK (*calcium carbonate*) mixed to a thick dough with boiled linseed or other oil. It is used to hold glass in windows and to even out surfaces before painting them.

Pylorus see Digestive system

Pyramid see Geometry

Pyridoxine see Vitamin

Pyrimidine (pi-RIM-ih-den) A pyrimidine is an organic compound. The molecule has four carbon and two nitrogen atoms in a six-sided ring. Pyrimidine rings are found in Vitamins B1, and B2, and folic acid.

Three pyrimidines—thymine, cytosine, and uracil—are present in the nucleic acids DNA (deoxyribonucleic acid) and RNA (ribonucleic acid). These acids occur in cell nuclei.

Organic structure of a pyrimidine molecule

The nucleic acid containing DNA, combined with protein, forms the dark-staining chromatin of a nucleus. Chromatin carries the GENES that determine inheritance of animal or plant characteristics. The nucleic acid RNA is made in the nucleus and acts as a messenger carrying instructions from the genes to particles in the cytoplasm called *ribosomes*. Ribosomes make the type of cellular parts and enzymes called for by the genes. J. C. K.

SEE ALSO: NUCLEOPROTEINS, PURINE

Iron pyrite crystals are usually cubic

Pyrite (PYE-rite) Pyrite is a common mineral found throughout the world. Because of its glinting, shiny-yellowish color, it has often been mistaken for gold, and is commonly called "fool's gold." It often occurs in veins of QUARTZ or in LIMESTONE.

The name pyrite is derived from the Greek word meaning "fire" because of the sparks which occur when it is struck with steel. Pyrite will also sustain fire, due to its sulfur content.

Pyrite is the commonest of the sulfide minerals. It is found associated with other sulfides, with oxides, and in quartz veins, in sedimentary and metamorphic rocks, in coal beds. It is also a replacement mineral found in fossils.

In some countries, where sulfur is not common, pyrite is used to obtain pure sulfur, but in the United States it is used commercially mainly for sulfuric acid. The formula for pyrite is FeS_2. V. V. N.

Pyroxene (pye-RAHK-seen) A scientist selected the name pyroxene from the Greek, *pyr* meaning "fire" and *xenos,* "stranger;" thus the name

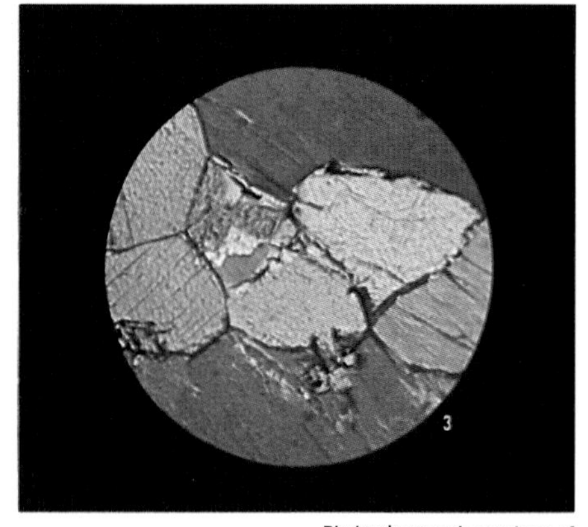

Photomicrograph courtesy of National Teaching Aids, Inc.

Pyroxene's large crystals show that it was formed deep in the earth.

means "stranger to fire." This is not characteristic, however, for the various pyroxenes are typically minerals of the igneous or melted rock group.

Pyroxene belongs to a group of minerals which show a cleavage angle of 87 degrees to 93 degrees parallel to the fundamental prism. Chemically the pyroxenes are *metasilicates*.

Pyroxene crystals are generally short, stout, complex prisms. They are common in basic igneous rocks, and may be developed in the earth by pressure and moderate heat, as in *gneisses, schists,* and *marble*. A common pyroxene is called augite. V.V.N.

Pythagoras (pih-THAGG-uh-russ) (582?-500?) Pythagoras was a Greek philosopher who was active about 530 B.C. Scarcely anything is known of Pythagoras' early life, but it is believed that he was born on the island of Samos.

He was important for having worked out a method of proving what is now known as the *Pythagorean theorem*. This theorem states that the square of the hypotenuse of a right-angled triangle is equal to the sum of the squares of the other two sides. D. H. J.

SEE ALSO: GEOMETRY

Python see Snakes

Pythagoras

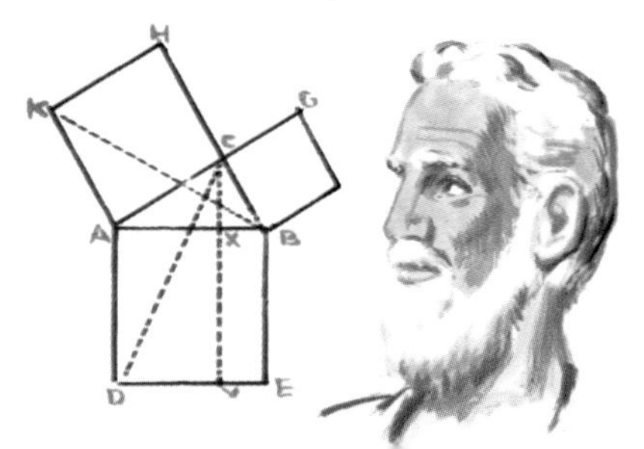

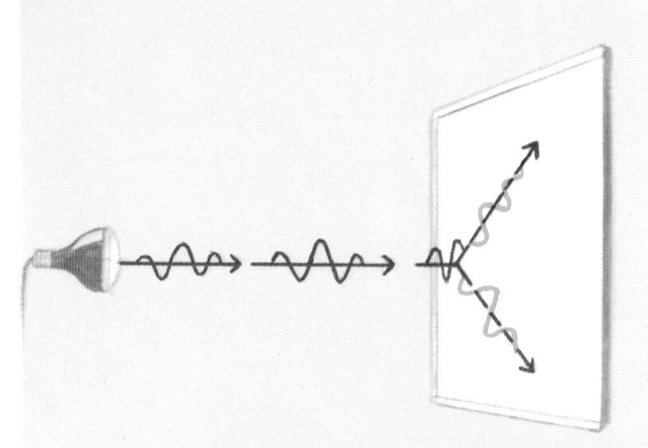

When a photon collides with an electron at the surface of a substance, the electron is excited into motion. This results in heat or electric current being produced, or a change in conductivity of the surface material, depending on the nature of the substance

Quadruplets see Multiple births

Quail Partridge is another name for quail. The BOBWHITE is a common North American quail. Of the sixty species of quail, only seven are found north of Mexico. The bodies of most quail are patterned in brown and white. Their coloring blends well into the background of their grassy natural habitat (PROTECTIVE COLORATION).

Although quail in southern United States are called partridges, the true partridges are Old World birds. They are heavier than quail and lack a toothlike projection on their beaks. Two species of true partridges have been introduced into the United States and are thriving.

Except for the bobwhite, other species of American quail have some kind of a crest or plume on the top of their heads. The most amusing topknot occurs on the *California* quail. Its plume is slender and looks like a single quotation mark poised on the top of its head. Quails are chicken-like and nest on the ground. They do not migrate. They are *monogamous* birds, having only one mate for life. J. C. K.

Quantum mechanics (KWANN-tum) The physical laws that describe the relationships of subatomic particles to RADIATION is called quantum mechanics. The primary concept is that energy moves into and out of matter in natural packets called *quanta*. A single packet is called a *quantum*.

As modern studies of the atom and its interaction with radiant energy developed, more and more differences between experimental results and the older theories used to explain them became apparent. The early theories were based on Newton's laws and the related wave laws and assumed that energy existed in wholly divisible, continuous waves.

Max Planck, professor of theoretical physics in Berlin, brought the issue to a head in 1900. Before him, many studies of energy transfer had been done. Materials were heated to glowing temperatures. This excitement of atoms or molecules of matter is called RADIATION. Black-surface objects were noted to be most satisfactory; other colors added confusing factors. When black materials are heated, their radiated energy depends solely on the temperature. Earlier scientists tried to explain the radiation rate by use of classical wave laws. Specifically, in the late 1800s Lord Rayleigh, Sir James Jeans, and others tried to apply these older mechanics theories and admitted that they did not succeed.

Finally in 1900, Planck used the data from black-body radiation to focus on how the atoms of matter radiate energy. The only formula he found to work had to start from the new assumption that atoms contain only *discrete* quantities, or quanta, of energy.

By 1905, Albert EINSTEIN called attention not only to Planck's issue but to certain recent experiments that he thought called for a new theory. He cited Edison's discovery of the "thermionic effect" (1883), Hertz' "photoelectric effect" (1887), and Leonard's work showing that energy of electrons varied with their frequency of emission (1902). All of these led him to theorize that there exist unit amounts of energy called *photons,* the size of which depends on the rate of vibration *(frequency)* of the subatomic particles emitting them. It could be expressed mathematically by merely three symbols, one of

In this electroluminescent wall, an electric current frees electrons, which strike atoms of the phosphor which then emit photons (bundles of light energy)

which was the "constant of proportionality." In honor of the original proponent, this constant was called Planck's Constant. Einstein's formula is: E=Hf (where *E* is the total energy of an emitted photon; *f* is the vibration rate; and *H* is Planck's Constant, 6.62 x 10^{-34} joule/sec).

In summary, Planck and Einstein held that even though any given kind of radiant energy travels through space in continuous waves, it is absorbed or emitted as photons in packet-like units or quanta.

Shortly after the quantum theory was first announced, Niels Bohr, a Danish physicist, was able to apply it further to form a new theory about atomic structure. Bohr's original atomic model has been modified, but even the latest theories still agree with the idea of energy quanta.

The quantum theory is currently being developed in three branches: quantum field theory, relativistic quantum mechanics, and non-relativistic quantum mechanics. The field theory deals with energy during the creation and destruction of elementary particles. The non-relativistic branch has to do with particles and their energies when at low velocities compared with light. The relativistic branch deals with velocities near and equal to that of light. DAB/MBC

SEE ALSO: LIGHT, PHOTON, RADIATION

Quarantine Quarantine is the isolation of persons, animals, or plants which have been exposed to communicable diseases. The quarantine period lasts for a time equal to the incubation period of the disease.

Quarry (KWAWR-ee) A quarry is an opening in the earth caused by removal of stone. Such rocks as limestone, marble, sandstone, and granite are obtained by the procedure known as *quarrying.*

Quarrying is accomplished by the methods of *explosion, "plug and feather,"* and *channeling.* Explosion is done with dynamite or gunpowder to open or clear large areas. The resulting rubble is of primary use for roads or for smelting limestone rock.

The other methods are used chiefly for quarrying building stone. Plug and feather refers to a wedge with two half cylindrical pieces fitting on either side which are placed in a series of drilled holes in rock. Hammering the wedge spreads the "feathers" to apply pressure, causing a splitting of the formation.

Channeling involves a locomotive-like vehicle on a track with mechanical chisels to channel or cut the rock. This represents modern mechanized quarrying. D. J. I.

Quarrying granite

Quartz Quartz is one of the most common minerals. It consists of *silicon dioxide,* or *silica.* It is found in many places and in many types of rock formations. Several varieties of quartz are used as gems. Others are building materials. Quartz is very hard.

There are many colors and many varieties of quartz. The color is due to other minerals and determines certain varieties. *Rock crystal* is pure, clear, transparent quartz. Purple quartz is called *amethyst.* These are crystalline varieties. *Agate* is an opaque type in which the color is distributed unevenly

J. Daniel Willems

ROCK CRYSTAL QUARTZ IN NATURAL STATE

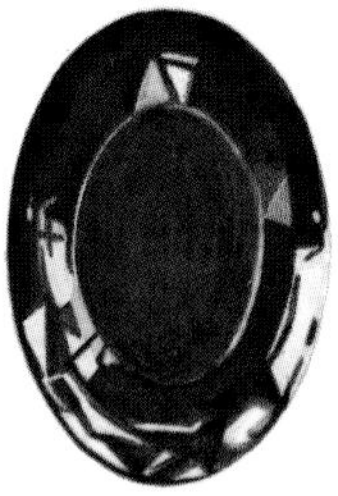

AMETHYST

CITRINE

QUARTZ IS A HEXAGONAL CRYSTAL. OTHER MINERALS PRESENT IN THE QUARTZ WILL PRODUCE COLOR, AS SHOWN IN THE POLISHED STONES

ROSE QUARTZ

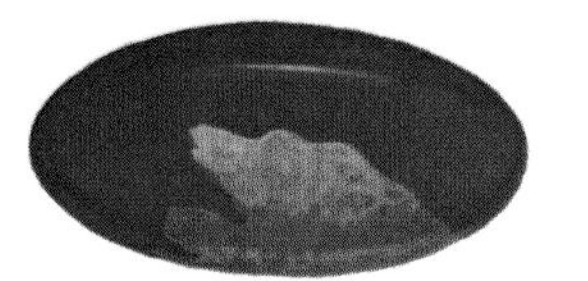

JASPER

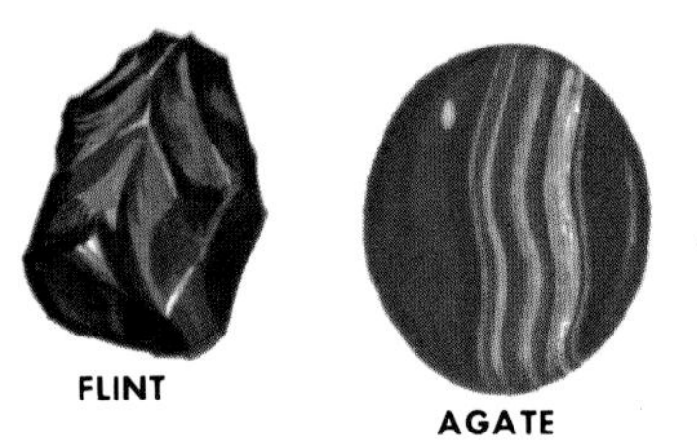

FLINT

AGATE

through its mass. Sometimes the color runs through in curved bands. In *moss agate* specimens, the color is arranged so that it looks as if moss or other vegetable matter has been "frozen" in the quartz. Agate, *carnelian,* and *onyx* are usually considered as special types of quartz—*chalcedony.* Chalcedony is the *massive* form of quartz. Other varieties include bloodstone, flint, jasper, chert, aventurine, and opal. C.L.K.

SEE ALSO: AGATE, AMETHYST, GEM, ONYX

Quartzite see Rocks

Quasar (KWAY-zar) Quasars, or quasi-stellar radio sources, are thought to be young galaxies. Quasars are strong radio sources. There are indications that quasars are moving at very great speeds.

The first quasar was discovered in 1963 by Marten Schmidt. Quasars are very far from the earth. They emit energy across much of the electromagnetic spectrum, strongest in the ultraviolet range. Quasars are extremely bright, but vary in intensity at an uneven rate. The fluctuations occur over short periods of time, indicating a small size. A.J.H.

Quaternary see Cenozoic Era, Geologic time table

Queen see Ants, Bees

Queen Anne's lace see Wild flowers

Quicklime see Lime

Quicksand Quicksand is a bed of very fine, powdery, wet sand. It may look solid, but it is like a thick fluid. It will not support anything heavy. Men, animals, trains, or automobiles can be swallowed up if they move onto quicksand.

Under quicksand there is usually a layer of clay. The clay keeps the water from draining away from the sand. Quicksand is often found at the mouths of rivers where fine sand has been deposited on clay. It can also be found around lakes or ponds if a hollow pocket in a clay shore holds it and keeps it wet.

Quicksand is very treacherous. There are

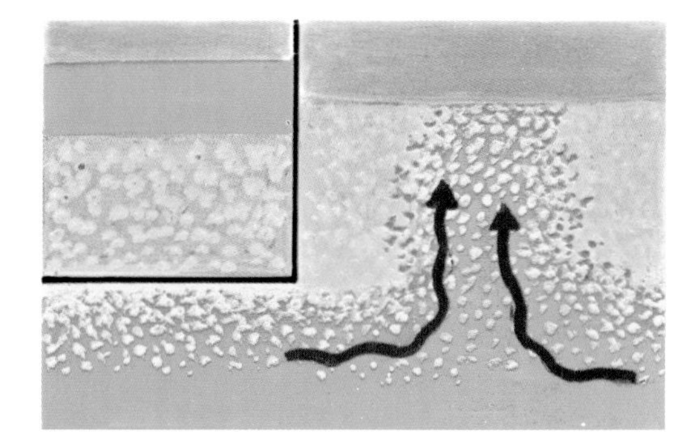

An underground spring that does not have enough outlets for the water may keep sand floating loosely. The upper left shows packed sand under still water, or water with outlets

many tales of people sinking into quicksand. This need not happen if the person stays calm and still. Taking special care not to move, the person will stop sinking when the quicksand reaches his armpits. Body weight then will balance the weight of displaced sand until help arrives. C.L.K.

SEE ALSO: GEOLOGY

Quicksilver see Mercury (element)

Quill see Feather

Quince Flowering quinces are popular garden shrubs that are among the first to blossom in the spring. These shrubs belong to the rose family and come from eastern Asia. The five-petaled, showy flowers bloom before or with the unfolding of the leaves. They make fine specimen plants and are also used for hedges. They are easily raised in most soils and are propagated by cuttings or layering.

Japonica is a variety known as dwarf Japanese quince. It is a low, spreading plant that grows about 3 feet (.9 meter) high and has red flowers.

Lagenaria is known as Japanese quince. It grows 4 to 6 feet (1.2 to 1.8 meters) tall and has spiny branches. Its flowers are scarlet or white, but some have pink flowers that turn red in the fall. It is the best flowering quince for hedges.

The hard, acid fruit called quince is related to the pear and apple. It is also a member of the rose family. The fruit is very tasty when it is cooked. M. R. L.

Flowering quince

Quinine (KWY-nyne) Quinine is a fever-reducing drug used in the treatment of MALARIA. It is a white, odorless, crystalline powder with a bitter taste. It comes from the bark of the *cinchona tree* originally found in South America. Because of the demand for quinine, the tree is now raised in the East Indies, Jamaica, Java, and other tropical countries. To prepare quinine, the bark is stripped from the trees and dried. It is then ground into a powder, from which the quinine is extracted.

Cinchona bark was used in early times by the Inca Indians of South America, who called it *quinaquina*. It was introduced in Europe in 1640, when it was used to cure the fever of the wife of the Peruvian Viceroy. She was Countess Cinchon, for whom the cinchona tree was named.

Before World War II, most quinine came from the Dutch East Indies. When the Dutch East Indies fell into Japanese hands, the supply of quinine for the Allied troops fighting in the tropics was cut off. It was necessary to develop synthetic drugs for the control of malaria, and *atabrine* became the best known.

Quinine is also used as a remedy for joint and muscle pain and for headaches, in the treatment of varicose veins, and as an appetite stimulant. M. R. L.

Quintuplets see Multiple births

Quinine is obtained from the cinchona tree

Rabbit The rabbit family includes both hares and rabbits. They are small, furry, gnawing mammals with long ears and short tails. They can run fast, taking great leaps with their long, powerful hind legs.

Rabbits and hares are alike, except for size and nesting habits. Rabbits are much smaller than hares. European ones usually have their babies in an underground burrow which they have dug themselves, or which another animal has dug. Their babies are blind and helpless, and have no fur when they are born. American hares rarely dig burrows. They usually have their babies out in the open or in a shady spot under a clump of bushes. Baby hares are well-developed when they are born.

There are several groups of jack rabbits found on the plains of North America. They are big hares about 28 inches (71.1 centimeters) long, weighing up to 10 pounds (4.5 kilograms). They have very long ears, very long hind legs, and are known for their speed. A jack rabbit may have as many as six litters each year.

The varying or snowshoe hare, found in the colder parts of northern North America, is white in winter and brown in summer. It sheds twice a year, growing a coat of brown in the spring and a coat of white in the fall. Its feet, which are long, broad, and heavily furred, serve as snowshoes in winter.

The arctic hare is a large white hare with short ears and legs and snowshoe feet. It feeds on mosses and grasses growing under the arctic snow.

Courtesy Society For Visual Education, Inc.

Snowshoe rabbit, or varying hare, is a true hare. Its coat, or *pelage*, changes color as the seasons change

Curtis J. Carley: U.S. Fish & Wildlife Service

The desert cottontail has the typical white underside to its tail.

James P. Rowan

Rabbits can be bred for a variety of fur colors.

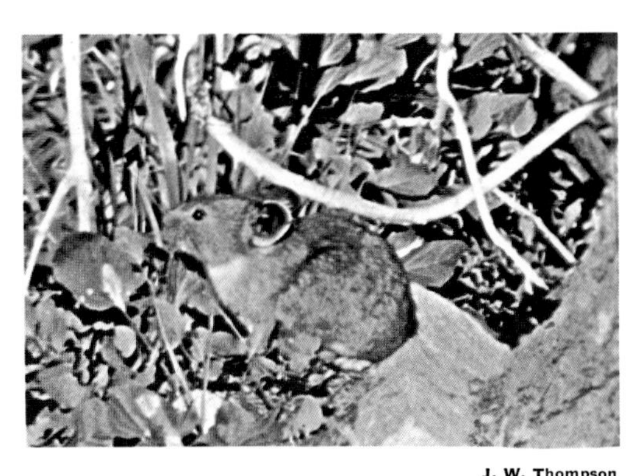

J. W. Thompson

Pika, a short-eared member of the rabbit family

F. A. Blashfield

Domestic albino white rabbit

Interesting members of the rabbit family are the *cony* or *pika,* living in colonies above the timberline in mountains in the Northern Hemisphere. They are small, brown animals weighing less than a pound (.5 kilogram). Their diet is grass and moss, which they store for winter.

The brown cottontail rabbit, common throughout North America, is easily identified by the white underside of its tail. It is a small rabbit, weighing about 2 or 3 pounds (.9 to 1.4 kilograms). Cottontails eat tender green plants, usually feeding in the early morning or late afternoon and spending the rest of the day under protective cover. The mother builds the nest in a shallow hole in the ground, lining it with bits of its fur. Several litters of two to six babies may be born during the spring and summer. D.J.A.

SEE ALSO: RODENTIA

Rabbit fever see Animal diseases, Rabbit

Rabi, Isador Isaac (1898-1953) Rabi, an Austrian-American physicist, discovered the radiations of atoms and found a process for measuring them. He was awarded the Nobel Prize in physics in 1944. He served as chairman of the Advisory Committee of the Atomic Energy Commission from 1952 to 1956.

Born in Rymanow, Austria, Rabi was brought to the United States as a young child. At the age of twenty-nine, he earned a Ph.D. at Columbia University, where he became a physics professor. During World War II he supervised the development of radar devices at the Radiation Laboratory of the Massachusetts Institute of Technology. He also served as consultant to the Los Alamos Atomic Bomb Laboratory.

Rabi is noted for his work in magnetism and QUANTUM MECHANICS. He developed and applied a new technique called the *resonance method* to research on the magnetic properties of atomic nuclei.

He has contributed to science journals and his book, *My Life and Times as a Physicist,* was published in 1960. Many honors have been awarded to him for his service to humanity. M. W. C.

Rabies Rabies is a disease found among wild and domestic animals. It is sometimes called *hydrophobia,* which means "fear of water," because rabies causes paralysis of throat muscles, and the victim, although thirsty, cannot swallow.

In *dumb rabies* the infected animal is listless, dull-eyed and unable to swallow. The voice is hoarse, the mouth hangs open and the jaw drips saliva. There is no indication of unfriendliness, and many times the disease is not recognized until infection has passed on through a break in the skin of the animal's handler. *Furious rabies* is easier to recognize because the infected animal, in addition to hoarseness and slobbering, wanders off and becomes violent.

Rabies among wild animals, fox, bats, skunks, and squirrels, is referred to as *sylvatic rabies.* In domestic animals it is known as *urban* rabies. All pets should be given anti-rabies vaccinations for protection of the pet and the owner. Health departments make every effort to curb the disease by vaccinating stray animals, and issuing dog licenses. This dread disease can be transmitted to any unvaccinated pet by wild animals.

The rabies' *virus* lives in the salivary glands of the infected animal and can be passed on to humans through a bite. The VIRUS travels by nerve trunks to the central nervous system where it finally causes death to the nerve cells. The period between the entry of the rabies' virus into the body and the first signs of the disease may be from four to eight weeks.

For humans exposed to rabies, both passive immunization and active immunization must be used. The latter involves 23 painful "shots," given over a 34-day period. G.A.D.

SEE ALSO: ANIMAL DISEASES; PASTEUR, LOUIS

Courtesy Society For Visual Education, Inc.

North American raccoon

Raccoon Raccoons are yellow-gray animals with broad heads tapering to pointed noses. They have black masks across their faces and around the eyes. Ears are medium sized. Tails are bushy and ringed with black. Raccoons are about the size of a cocker spaniel and have short, compact bodies. Except for the pandas in Asia, members of the raccoon family live only in the New World.

Raccoons are *plantigrades.* This means that they walk upon the whole foot. There is no hair on the soles of the feet. Claws are curved but not *retractile.*

Although raccoons are members of the order Carnivora, they are not true CARNIVORES or meat eaters. They are OMNIVORES and eat a wide variety of food such as corn, fruit, fish, small mammals, birds, and eggs. They are thought to be clean animals because they wash their food before eating. This is only partly true. In captivity, they do appear to wash food, but this activity is probably an expression of an aquatic hunting instinct.

Raccoons build nests in hollow trees and have five or six young in the late spring of each year. The young resemble their parents. Raccoons travel in family groups. Rarely is one seen alone. Most of their activity takes place at night. During the day, they take refuge in tree hollows. However, raccoons are not *arboreal* because they do not hunt or feed in trees. When winter comes, they *hibernate.* J. C. K.

Race Race is a *subdivision* of a species. It is made up of animals or plants, usually of one locality, having a combination of physical characteristics, such as appearance or bodily structure, which distinguishes them from others of the species. These characteristics can be inherited.

SEE: EVOLUTION OF MAN, HUMAN BEING

Radar Radar is an electronic system that permits man to see objects at great distances regardless of darkness or bad weather. It is used to direct both air and sea traffic, and for detection and identification of unknown ships and aircraft.

Sound waves bouncing off hillsides or tunnel walls create an echo. Radar works in the same way by sending out short *pulses* of radio energy which bounce off objects in their path and return to the sender as a type of echo. The reflected impulses are shown on a screen, like that of a television set, as spots of light, or *blips.*

Most radar sets have six important parts: the *modulator,* which turns the transmitter on to send a pulse and off to receive an echo; the *transmitter,* which sends the very short, or *microwave,* pulses; the *antenna,* which focuses the pulses into a narrow beam and also receives the echoing signals; the *duplexer,* which, as a switching device, connects first the transmitter and then the receiver to the antenna; the *receiver,* which is a listening and amplifying device to strengthen weak echoes so that they will show on the radar screen; and the *indicator,* which displays the blips to the operator on its screen.

KINDS OF INDICATORS

While most radar sets work in the same way, there are several types of indicators, each designed for a particular job. The *Plan Position Indicator,* or PPI, is the most common type. It has a round screen with a compass scale around the outside. On this screen a beam of light, representing the beam of radar pulses being sent out of the antenna, rotates like the second hand of a clock. As this beam, or *trace,* sweeps around the screen, the blips appear as spots of light when it passes. The distance of the objects they represent is determined by their distance on the screen from the center, which is the station. The screen usually has rings showing distance from the center. Another type of indicator is the *Range Height Indicator,* or RHI, which measures the height of objects such as airplanes. The RHI has a trace that sweeps up and down and shows the range and height of an object in one given direction. It is used to assist pilots in

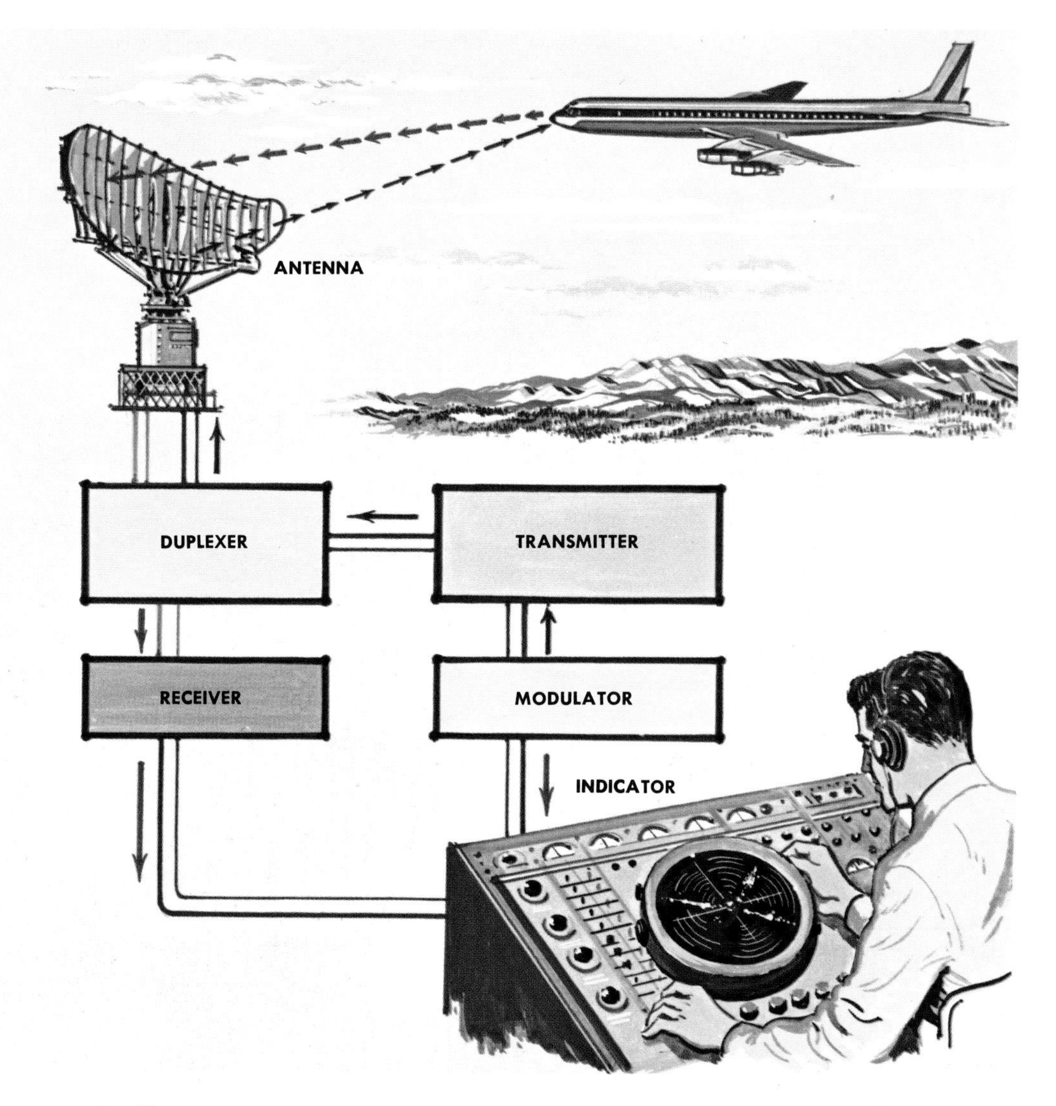

instrument landings.

The A-scope and B-scope indicators give more details about the objects they detect, such as the number of aircraft in a formation.

SPECIAL USES OF RADAR

Police forces use *Doppler,* or *Continuous Wave,* radar to determine the speed of passing automobiles. This type of radar sends out continuous radio waves instead of pulses. The rate of vibrations, or frequency, of the returning echoes is different from the frequency of the transmitted signal, and this difference is measured to obtain the speed of the target.

The first use of radar for measuring distance was in 1934. Today, very sensitive radar devices are used to map the surface of Venus. Radar devices are used by police to enforce speed laws. All major airports use radar to control air traffic during landings and departures. The weather bureau uses radar in predicting weather and for tracking storms. R.J.J.

SEE ALSO: INSTRUMENT LANDING SYSTEM

Radial symmetry see Animals, classification of

Radiant energy Radiant energy is ENERGY that travels in the form of electromagnetic waves. These waves are classified—in order of decreasing wave length—as *radiowaves, infrared waves, visible light, ultraviolet rays, X rays, and gamma rays.*

SEE ALSO: RADIATION

Conversion Factors to Metric Measurement

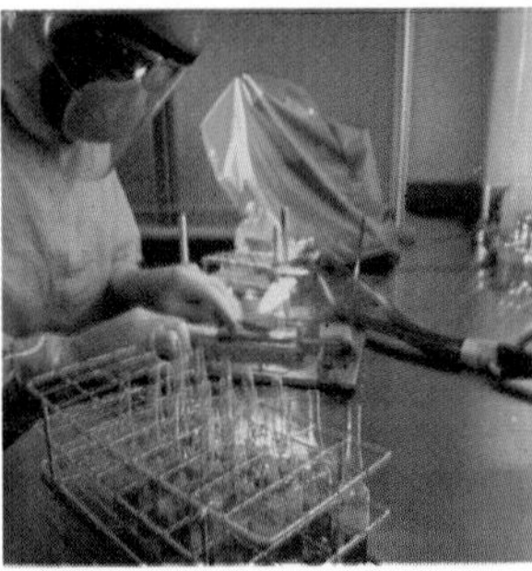

Length

1 inch = 25.4 millimeters (mm) exactly

1 inch = 2.54 centimeters (cm) exactly

1 foot = 0.3048 meters (m) exactly

1 yard = 0.9144 meters (m) exactly

1 mile = 1.609344 kilometers (km) exactly

Area

1 square inch = 6.4516 square centimeters (cm^2) exactly

1 square foot = 0.092903 square meters (m^2)

1 square yard = 0.836127 square meters (m^2)

1 square acre = 0.404686 hectares (ha)

1 square mile = 2.58999 square kilometers (km^2)

Cubic Measure

1 cubic inch = 16.387064 cubic centimeters (cm^3) exactly

1 cubic foot = 0.0283168 cubic meters (m^3)

1 cubic yard = 0.764555 cubic meters (m^3)

US Liquid Measure

1 fluid ounce = 29.5735 milliliters (ml)

1 fluid ounce = 0.2957 deciliters (dl)

1 pint = 0.473176 liters (l)

1 gallon = 3.78541 liters (l)

US Dry Measure

1 pint = 0.550610 liters (l)

1 bushel = 35.2391 liters (l)

Weight

1 grain = 0.0647989 grams (g)

1 ounce = 28.3495 grams (g)

1 pound = 0.453592 kilograms (kg)

1 short ton = 0.907185 metric tons (t)

1 UK ton = 1.01605 metric tons (t)

Temperature

To convert Fahrenheit to Centigrade (Celsius) complete the following equation. $(F^\circ - 32) \times 5 \div 9 = C^\circ$